ConnectZone.org

Building connectedness in schools

by

Bev Ogilvie

Published by InsideOut Media

Cover design and layout by Lewis Evans
lewis@lewisevans.net

Library and Archives Canada Cataloguing in Publication

Ogilvie, Bev, 1953-, author
    ConnectZone.org: building connectedness in schools / by Bev Ogilvie

ISBN: 978-0-9879291-6-7 (pbk.)

    1. Home and school. 2. Community and school. 3. Parent-teacher relationships. I. Title.

LC225.O35 2014   371.19'2   C2014-900864-3

Printed in Canada
♻
on recycled paper
VICTORIA BINDERY

www.victoriabindery.com
Victoria, BC

10 9 8 7 6 5 4 3

In memory of Dr Naomi Serrano

1936-2008

teacher, psychologist, mentor

You invited me to exist in your presence
so that I could exist in mine.

ConnectZones defined

ConnectZones have an important purpose of creating and maintaining safe, warm, welcoming, supportive, inclusive places.

They are environments of human connection, open communication, collaboration, trust, compassion and tolerance.

They are nurturing communities of care, where children, adolescents and adults are attended to, valued and accepted.

ConnectZones foster a sense of rootedness, harmony, belonging and connection.

They allow for meaningful relationships, physical and emotional safety, security, exploration, self-expression, growth and maturation.

ConnectZone.org

Building connectedness in schools

Contents

Part 2. Finding the connector in you

Part 3. Creating a ConnectZone: a connected school community

About the author

Bev Ogilvie

A District Counsellor with the Burnaby School District, Associate Professor with City University, temporary instructor with Vancouver Island University, and a senior instructor with the Crisis Prevention Institute, Bev received her Master of Arts in Counselling Psychology Degree from the University of British Columbia (UBC). She has 30 years of professional teaching experience in public schools as well as in colleges and universities. She is a Registered Clinical Counsellor, a member of the British Columbia School Counsellors' Association, the National Association of School Psychologists, and the BC School Centered Mental Health Coalition. Bev was awarded the 2009-2010 British Columbia Registered Clinical Counsellor Professional Care Award for exhibiting special creativity and effectiveness in providing counselling and professional care. She is an author, researcher, and workshop facilitator who embraces integrated developmental approaches, both in her leadership role in the school community and in her personal life.

Contributors

Lis Kroeker

A faculty member of the Neufeld Institute, Lis has been working in the education system for 24 years. Her experience includes classroom teaching, working with families with special needs, supporting students with troubling behaviours, working as a school counsellor at the elementary and middle-school levels, and working as a district resource teacher. Lis teaches Special Education courses at the post-secondary level and coordinates the Teacher Post-Degree Diploma in Special Education at Vancouver Island University. She is a mother of two and brings with her a deep sense of compassion and a strong belief in the ability of the attachment-based developmental approach to change the lives of children. She also has extensive experience providing in-service training to teachers and teachers-in-training, and has worked with teams of educators and parents of children who are struggling. She provides educational consulting and counselling through her private practice.

Sarah Coleborn

Born in England, Sarah immigrated to Vancouver, BC at the age of 12 and made the Vancouver area her home. She has worked for the Burnaby School District for 10 years, supporting students with special needs and those considered to be 'at risk'. For the past six years, Sarah has been working at an inner-city school that has a high proportion of students with refugee status. There, she implements the attachment-based developmental approach in her work with all children. Sarah has studied Dr Neufeld's attachment-based developmental approach and has taken his Power to Parent, Power to Teach and Neufeld Intensive I courses. Sarah works as a behavioural interventionist with students with ASD (Autism Spectrum Disorder) in Verbal Applied Behaviour Analysis. At her home, close to the school where she works, Sarah (a mother and step-mother to five children) opens her heart and her home to children with special needs and provides respite care. Sarah is invested in the process of helping stuck children get 'unstuck', and helping them to realize their emotional and academic potential.

Steve Cairns

A retired school administrator, Steve has had a 35-year career in public education with School District #41 Burnaby. Steve received his Bachelor of Arts from Simon Fraser University and his Master of Education from City University. He is the recipient of the City of Burnaby Local Hero Award for Outstanding Contribution to the Community and co-author of *Brain Fit 2002,* as well as a published author in several professional publications. Steve is a former Administrative Designate to BC Fast ForWord Consortium, Director of Village Elders and Leaders and Co-Founder of Collaborative for the Study of Connectedness in School Communities.

Rebecca Christofferson

Rebecca has a strong desire to shift family health back to the centre of Canadian values and society. In 1996, she had the honour of graduating on Qu'wut'sun land from Island University's Arts One First Nations program. Inspired by indigenous models of mental health, she pursued an education in arts-based empowerment. During her 11-year career in art therapy, she worked with many First Nations people in urban aboriginal settings, as well as on reservations. For seven years, Rebecca developed and facilitated aboriginal therapeutic services for families dealing with addictions, attachment disorders, mental health issues, abuse and residential school trauma. Her career has focused on supporting individuals and families towards empowerment through strengthening attachments, community connections, cultural awareness, and ceremonial healing.

Wade Wilson

Wade was raised in the small town of Hazelton, BC, where he developed a love of animals, athletics, nature and artistic expression. Upon graduating, he moved to Vancouver to pursue a teaching career. He received his BA in English Literature and teaching certificate from Simon Fraser University. Having achieved his qualifications, Wade worked intensely with a wide variety of special needs children in the Burnaby School District as an Educational Assistant. This work influenced his approach when he moved on to teach in mainstream classes. He taught English, Physical Education and Information Technology in various schools throughout the UK, before returning to Canada, where his first assignment was teaching the Bridge Program at Burnaby Central. This program was designed to transition at-risk behaviourally-challenged students into high school. After two-and-a-half years in the Bridge Program, he now teaches English, full time, throughout the Burnaby School District.

Fran De Tracie

A graduate of the BC government care program, Fran has spent the last nine years as a school custodian. She has 15 years' experience as a school-based youth and child care counsellor and two years as a therapeutic foster parent. For 10 years, Fran worked in group homes in the Vancouver area and spent two years as a Downtown Eastside parks youth coordinator. Fran also worked for 10 years as a shop steward in the food industry and for two years as a representative on the Vancouver and District Labour Council.

Troy Closs

A father of five, Troy has 15 years of experience in the care industry. Troy's educational background is in recreation and physical education. Upon completion of his formal education in 1992 (Recreation and Leisure Studies, Physical Education), Troy worked as a special needs educator for the Burnaby School Board. He began working at his current school, Morley Elementary, in 2004.

Dave Rawnsley

Dave is the Principal at Byrne Creek Secondary School and the 2012 award-winner of the prestigious ASCD Whole Child Award. As a teacher and administrator in the Burnaby School District over the past 14 years, Dave has worked to create a culture of care, compassion and creativity in his classrooms and school. He has been inspired by many students and colleagues throughout his career and considers himself very lucky to be working alongside amazing people in the Burnaby School District. Dave completed his Bachelor of Arts degree from Mount Allison University in Sackville, New Brunswick before returning to BC to complete his Bachelor of Education at UBC and his Masters of Education at Simon Fraser University (SFU). Dave is happily married to Sheila, an elementary teacher in Burnaby, and is the proud father of two children.

Gayle Hernandez

Gayle has been a teacher in the Burnaby School District since 1993. Early Childhood Education (ECE) is her passion; families and children the heart of her practice. She holds a Masters Degree from UBC, with an ECE specialization. For her Masters Degree, she explored ways to embrace familial diversity in a cultural and multilingual kindergarten classroom, as well as ways to build and bridge relationships with parents through the *Learning Together* program. Over the years, Gayle has written and presented workshops, as well as mentoring student teachers. Gayle facilitated the Burnaby School District Early Learning Network for 10 years, serving on the Report Card, Ready Set Learn, Early Learning and Language Arts committees. She completed Burnaby's leadership program and, for four years, supervised a school site during Summer Session. She has been a guest on a USA radio show, talking about inclusion of children.

Acknowledgements

I am indebted to Dr Gordon Neufeld, a highly respected clinical psychologist and leading interpreter of the developmental paradigm. Dr Neufeld, best known for his breakthrough insights on attachment and aggression, has created a coherent and powerful working model of development that is highly effective for parents and professionals alike. His reputation for making sense of complex problems and for opening doors to change is widely acknowledged and respected.

I also greatly value the groundbreaking approach of Dr Ross Greene (www.livesinthebalance.org), a clinical psychologist, distinguished clinician and pioneer in working with behaviourally challenged children. Drawing on research from the neurosciences, Dr Greene offers an innovative conceptual framework for understanding the difficulties of children with behavioural challenges. He gives teachers and parents realistic strategies and information on how to radically improve interactions with challenging children. Greene's work, like Neufeld's, explains why traditional school discipline isn't effective with disruptive children. Both Greene and Neufeld, backed by years of experience and research, write with a powerful sense of hope and achievable change.

As well, I honour the legacy of Peter Benson (www.searchinstitute. org/sparks), a social scientist by vocation. His innovative, research-based framework transformed complex scientific insights into a compelling, clear and concrete vision of what each person could do to champion justice and compassion. Benson is one of the world's leading authorities on positive human development and social change, and his Developmental Assets approach to understanding and strengthening positive youth development is recognized worldwide. Closely aligning with Benson, I strongly believe that all children are our children, that adults have the power within themselves to help ignite the hidden strengths of children and youth, build their assets and change their lives. It was Benson who coined the term 'sparks' to describe passions and interests that engender purpose, focus, joy and energy, and that are good and useful for the world. Like Benson, I emphasize authentic adult relationships as critical for discovering and nurturing sparks, for unleashing human capacity and spirit, and for creating a better world.

Furthermore, I have been inspired by the work of Daniel Siegel, Brené Brown and Bruce Perry, who have shown me how vital and humanizing our capacity to care really is. Their message—that connection gives purpose and meaning to our lives—is a theme that remains paramount for me. Siegel, like Neufeld, amplifies the vital importance of creating secure and safe attachments between a child and his or her caregivers. Siegel, a neuro-psychiatrist, reminds us that human connections shape neural connections and that attachment relationships may serve to create the central foundation from which the mind develops. Being compassionate to others and to ourselves is a natural outcome of the healthy development of the mind.

Brown is an award-winning professor at the University of Houston, whose ground-breaking research on vulnerability has magnified, for me, how resilient and resourceful I am. She has inspired me to chart a new course, one that has helped me to gain perspective on how to 'dare greatly' and to be more courageous, self-compassionate and determined to be the author of my own life. I aspire to realize my potential as a connector, as well as my sense of agency and responsibility.

Perry, a renowned child-psychiatrist, neuro-scientist and professor of psychiatry at Northwestern University School of Medicine in Chicago, is dedicated to improving the lives of at-risk, vulnerable children and to exploring the crucially important role that love, support and encouragement play in all our lives. I admire his life-long dedication to understanding how trauma affects children and to developing innovative ways to help those raised with chaos, threat and abuse to recover. He has helped those of us who work with troubled youth to understand the critical impact of early experiences on children's lives, and how traumatic experience marks them, affecting their personalities and their capacity for physical and emotional growth.

Informed by Dr Neufeld's model for understanding child development, Benson's exploration of what kids need to succeed, and Greene's practical approach to understanding and guiding troubled and troubling students, this book applies developmental attachment approaches to the education system. Separate chapters are dedicated to the discussion of salient themes, many of them drawing on the work of the aforementioned psychologists, interspersed with my own perspectives. Implications for educational practice are explored throughout the book and stories provide contextual examples of what it means to 'walk the talk of connectedness in schools'.

Finally, I would like to acknowledge and send my deepest gratitude to the contributing authors, particularly for their unwavering belief in this project; to Steve Cairns for his incredible contribution and tireless editing; to Lewis Evans for editing, design and production; and to Lis Kroeker and Jan Chow for their work on the wiki sites. Thank you for making this happen!

Part 1. Understanding connectedness

1. Introduction

This book was written to inspire a social movement that champions a culture in which connectedness is valued above all—a movement that builds the most important organization of all: the family. As author and contributors, our desire is to win hearts and minds, to inspire people to get back to the basics—to their hearts—to better understand the nature and power of relationships and to connect with each other.

ConnectZone.org: Building connectedness in schools is about the need to make a paradigm shift by challenging the status quo and changing many of the policies and practices that exist in our education system. Although educators take great pride in the notion of working together to explore the possibilities for helping children to succeed in school, I have never been more concerned about how disconnected we are from each other. While many educators possess the vision and the drive to build connectedness in their school communities and are making conscious efforts to do so, responses continue to be reactionary, and preventative practices non-relational in nature. While schools are being magnified as social hubs, resulting in powerful learning experiences for students and increased opportunities to strengthen the fabric of community, they are viewed by many as castles with draw bridges—as closed systems with impenetrable walls. Educators are expressing discouragement with the erosion of their social status, and are weighted down with government-created curricula and a system obsessed with getting results. Educators feel disconnected for many reasons, including:

a. a growing culture of disengagement and blame in schools, due to hardworking, talented people being excluded, their creative ideas downplayed and their innovation ignored;

b. power in the hands of a few, with little accountability;

c. adults in positions of authority, habituated to ways of interacting that are often disrespectful, yet easily justified and rationalized by them.

d. leaders not living up to the values they preach; and

e. dedicated staff becoming frustrated and apathetic, due to their belief that systemic change is not possible.

Although I have painted a rather negative picture of schools, I remain extremely hopeful that, through teamwork and a focus on connectedness, we can right the ship. Research about connectedness reveals the following:

1. We are the most social of all species and we need warm, human connections to develop and live in a healthy manner.

2. There are positive outcomes to school connectedness, with students believing that adults and peers care about them as individuals and about their learning.

3. Connectedness, a measure of resilience, leads to better physical and emotional health.

4. Connectedness, when successfully practised in schools, reduces the prevalence of deviant and delinquent behaviour; leads to higher academic motivation and grade point average; promotes the development of supportive relationships with peers and teachers; and generates more positive perceptions of the overall school climate.

5. Human connections grow and shape the developing brain, and impact self-regulation.

6. Compassion can be taught in the classroom through example and practice.

7. Teaching compassion in schools can help children thrive.

8. Children who have secure attachments and who feel loved tend to be happier and more resilient over their lifespan.

9. Too much screen time (time spent with phones, televisions, computers, video games) is resulting in less time for children to learn empathy and in less emotional connectedness overall.

10. Empathy is threatened in the modern world due to too little time being spent on face-to-face interactions.

It's time to make a real difference. It's time to open doors and break down walls to promote and practise connectedness in school communities. Doing the right thing means purposefully and intentionally creating and maintaining 'ConnectZones' that are safe, warm, welcoming, supportive inclusive places. It means making schools 'human' places to be, not just safe places.

Connectedness in schools fosters appreciation and honour for each other. It involves adults taking the lead in children's lives and placing them in high esteem. An educator needs to be the type of person with whom children can totally be themselves, a 'safe place' where children are seen and heard and where they can share heartfelt feelings. Educators need to let children know that they really matter and that we are truly happy they exist.

This book pays tribute to catalysts of connection, including those who have contributed to its content and who 'walk the talk' in schools. It is our intention that, through vignettes of celebration, this book will not prescribe but, instead, will inform and open your eyes to the many wonderful things that educators are already doing. We hope it provides a bridge between theory and practice, while making connections at a level that inspires positive, caring action.

Finally, this book will enable educators—as connectors and protectors—to find a place within, where responsibility for children and each other is taken. As it informs educators of the merits of connectedness in schools, this book will touch you deep within your core. It will encourage you to give yourself permission to walk the path of connectedness that you intuitively know is the right one to follow.

2. Defining connectedness

The best and most beautiful things
in the world cannot be seen or even touched.
They must be felt with the heart.

—Helen Keller

All mammals are genetically designed to care and be cared for. We have evolved to be good to others; cooperation is in our DNA, and the essential nature of humans is to care.

Connection is why we are here. Human connection is key to the human condition. It is what gives purpose and meaning to our lives. Connection is defined as "the energy that is created between people when they feel seen, heard and valued; when they can give and receive without judgement. Belonging is the innate human desire to be part of something larger than us."[1]

Connection brings empathy

Connection allows one to be receptive to the feelings of others. Empathy, connecting with the emotion that someone else is experiencing, is the best reminder that we are not alone. Empathy, and the caring it enables, is an essential part of human health. We live our lives in relationships and it is in our nature to nurture and be nurtured. Caring allows us to live longer and be happier.[2]

Compassion and connection—the very things that give purpose and meaning to our lives—can only be learned if they are experienced.[3]

---

1   Brown, 2012, p145
2   Perry, 2010
3   Brown, 2012, p219

Human beings have to learn how to become humane. We cannot experience empathy if we are not connecting. Empathy requires relational interaction. It *is* connection. We develop empathy from receiving it or witnessing it. The essence of empathy is the ability to stand in another's shoes, to see and feel the world from other points of view. It helps us realize that our experience is human and that there is power in 'we'.

Empathy promotes health, creativity, intelligence and productivity. It encourages us to take on new perspectives, to be better problem-solvers by bringing out our humility and inclusiveness. In contrast, apathy and a lack of empathy contribute to individual and social dysfunction, inhumane ideologies and brutal actions.

Nurture calls

We are born for love; we need to practise love as we grow through different social experiences so that we can give it back in abundance. The brain becomes what it does most frequently. Healthy brain development is utterly reliant on empathetic nurturing. If we don't practise empathy, we cannot become more empathetic. If we don't interact with people, we cannot improve our connections to them.

The sobering reality, however, is that there is growing evidence that we've lost our humanity. The economy has become the most important thing in our lives. Expressed empathy has been eroded due to rapid changes in our society. Advances in technology, high mobility of our populations, and the ongoing instability of families and communities have contributed to a reduction in the quantity and quality of human interactions, thereby hindering the development of our capacity for compassion. Overall, we are less trusting, have fewer close relationships, spend less time socializing, and tend to keep our children in structured activities that reduce the time they spend with friends and family. As a result, a number of things have declined:[4]

---

4   Perry, 2010, pp288-292

a. Religious participation

b. Amount of financial support we give to charities

c. Participation in political activities, as evidenced by declining voter populace

d. Membership in clubs or groups that require face-to-face participation.

e. Time children spend playing freely in unstructured activities (decreased by one third between 1981 and 2003)

f. Children playing outside, usually with other children (cut in half between 1981 and 1997)

g. Overall time available in schools for social activity

h. Freedom for children to roam

i. Physical affection towards children, which is important for their health and growth

j. Time spent by children in face-to-face interactions building relationships (now one-twenty-fourth the time spent on this by our hunter–gatherer ancestors).

All in all, children and adults today seem to be in deep 'attachment'[5] with their technological devices, distracted by the media and in isolation. Even though computer games and the Internet are more interactive than watching television, these activities still cannot provide the social engagement of face-to-face interaction and playing. This book delves into what we can do about these alarming trends of disintegrating social fabric that threaten our connection to each other. It highlights the importance of schools becoming 'ConnectZones' to help children, youth and adults feel a sense of belonging and significance.

---

5   Attachment is an emotional bond, a psychological connectedness. It is strong feelings of affection or loyalty for someone or something. It is a feeling that binds one to a person, thing, cause or ideal. The central theme of attachment theory is that primary caregivers need to be available and responsive to the infant in order for him/her to develop a sense of security. Attachment keeps infants and children close to their caregivers and provides children with a secure base from which they can safely venture forth and explore their environment. How a child is attached to his/her caregivers can significantly influence childhood and subsequent relationships.

When humans are born, they form attachments as a means of survival.[6] Children come to trust caregivers who provide for their physical needs. During their first year of life, children interpret relationships through their senses. They want to be with those with whom they are attached, connected to them visually and through smell, touch and taste. Without this proximity, they would literally die.

By age 2, once the brain is capable of understanding more complex dimensions of human interactions, children figure out that one way to keep a parent close is to become like the parent. They imitate, emulate and look for similarities between themselves and their caregivers. They walk like their caregivers, talk like them and want to be like them. Toddlers understand that they are part of a family or community by seeing what they have in common with their caregivers.

By age 3, a child starts to explore what it means to belong or hold on to mommy and daddy (or whoever the caregiver is) in several ways. They look for signs of loyalty and belonging from their caregivers. Much of the focus is on 'who are my people', and the instincts to serve and obey surface here. At this stage, attachment begins to influence the formation of the child's identity.

By age 4, children develop a sense of belonging through sameness and witnessing acts of loyalty. They begin to explore their uniqueness and significance. They understand that mommy and daddy hold close that which they hold dear. With closeness, the personality takes on a sweet tone. Children look to their caregivers for help in creating their unique roles and importance in the family or community. They seek approval and confirmation that they are significant to their caregivers.

By age 5, children gain the ability to understand what love means. Now that the limbic system has developed, they experience a deep, heartfelt relationship at a whole new level. Adults can feel the unbridled affection when children say "I love you." Children are full of love and often display it by drawing hearts on everything.

---

6   Neufeld, 2005

By age 6, it will occur to a child that to matter is to be seen and heard in a psychological way, deeply understood and known. A child wants to share what is in his/her heart. As Neufeld said, "Secrets will not divide...[the child] has become rooted in my garden."

The following stories illustrate how Rebecca focused on Neufeld's model of six developmental roots of healthy human attachment to establish connection with her students. It reminds us of what relationship looks like, how children are meant to attach to adults and that if we do not cultivate connections with children, we are not going to be able to do our jobs as parents and educators.

Roots of attachment: an art therapist's perspective
by Rebecca Christofferson

Through my work as an art therapist, I have worked with many children who have not had their attachment needs met. I work from the perspective that it is best to assess what is missing—what developmental attachment need is not being met. Then, I put my attention on how to meet these attachment needs and form relationships with children.

Senses

When I find a student closed off and hard to reach, I start with the senses. A pre-teen refugee from Africa refused to work with anyone involved with the Ministry of Child and Family Services. She was distrustful of authority and walked out of meetings as soon as anyone began asking her questions about her home life. She agreed, however, to join me for lunch and, at our next meeting, enjoyed the process of deciding what she was going to eat. For the next 10 months, our meetings were accompanied by sushi. With each session, our attachment grew a little stronger. After a few sessions, she began allowing me to help her problem-solve any social challenges she was having at the school. She then brought me poems, homework, and exciting things she was learning. Soon, I was allowed to hear her sadness, dreams and anger.

Sameness

Children look for physical similarities, similar interests and talents—anything that connects them to the group. This is a wonderful place to start a relationship with a teen. I used to run a social skills group at a youth detention centre. My first few sessions were not well attended. The youth had no interest in learning social skills. However, I continued to look for entry points into their lives—places where we were the same so we could understand each other. They soon asked me to bring in certain songs that they did not have access to in the detention centre. These songs were based in hip-hop culture, which I am also invested in. I spent time learning about the particular groups and rappers that were important to them. Soon, they trusted me enough to share how the songs were significant in their lives. These discussions provided an opportunity for me to model and educate them in non-violent communication. I was able to have them observe what they heard, talk about the feelings, and listen respectfully to each other. They allowed me to bring in more positive hip-hop songs that stimulated critical thinking discussions.

Belonging and loyalty

I worked in an urban aboriginal setting for many years and, as a white woman, I felt I did not belong. However, I have never felt more loyal to another work place. I still go to their yearly pow-wows to check in with staff and former clients. It is in the cultural framework of a group, school or family that people find a home.

In an attempt to provide youth with an opportunity to feel part of their heritage, the centre started a traditional canoe journey. A few months before our first canoe journey, a 17-year-old Cree girl began accompanying a boy who had been coming for over a year. She had run away from home to escape the parental addiction, neglect and physical violence she experienced during her childhood. This boy came to represent the only family she had, so it was easy for her to slip into a crystal meth addiction under his influence. She often expressed concern about her crystal meth use and made many attempts to quit. However, she was extremely attached to him and was unable to quit while he was still using. She decided that the canoe journey would be a good way to get away from the drug for a week, and she tried desperately to convince him to come on the journey with her. On the day we left, he backed out, so she had to make a quick decision about whether to come or not. She found the courage to come on the journey, but was worried that her decision to do so would make him mad enough to break up with her.

While on the trip, she struggled to keep up with the pace of paddling. But, with encouragement from the group, she persevered and paddled through the discomfort. She worked hard to learn some of the paddling songs and enjoyed the evening circles where elders shared songs around the fire. The group of paddlers in her canoe gave her a nickname and complimented her on some of her better qualities. On the last three days of the trip, she shared dreams she had during the night where an eagle had given her some information about who she was and where she belonged.

She returned from the trip committed to engaging in more cultural activities. Throughout the next few months, I saw her at pow-wows, aboriginal youth events and sweat lodges. She often took crystal meth and was still in and out of the relationship with her boyfriend. However, she stayed in touch with her aboriginal cultural group. Over the years, the periods when she was clean became longer and longer until she was eventually able to break up with the boyfriend and quit crystal meth.

Significance

One of my favourite jobs as an art therapist was managing the expressive art therapy department of a camp for children with learning disabilities. One 11-year-old boy struggled with language processing and had developed depression and low self-esteem. When he first started coming to camp, he would not participate in group games and activities. I ate meals with him outside the mess hall because he was scared of being hassled during meal times. I worked with him to find something that he liked and, through his fog of depression, we discovered that he enjoyed setting the tables before meals. Each day, we would set up the mess hall in preparation for meals, and then leave to eat outside when everyone began to arrive. I mentioned that the other kids would probably like to know who was doing such a nice thing for the whole camp. He allowed me to make an announcement after a meal, and he watched from outside as all the children clapped in his honour. We had a section of the recreation hall set aside where each student had a bag in which people could put nice messages. He began getting 'thank yous' from staff and students. He slowly began participating in camp activities until, eventually, to my surprise, he decided to start attending the drama club. I spent most of the last night of camp in tears of pride as I watched him perform with his club at our celebration. Towards the end of the evening, I gave him a necklace that said 'courage' on it. I told him to take it home to remind him that he was important to everyone at the camp.

Love

I worked for a transition house for women and children living in or leaving abusive relationships. While at the centre, a challenging 5-year-old girl, who witnessed and experienced violence at the hands of her father, was referred to me. As a result of the violence, she had developed defiant behaviour. She, along with her mother and brother, still lived with the father when we started therapy. The first session saw paint flying across my room, paper-shredding, and high-pitched shrieking. I worked hard to contain the art materials and counselling relationship so that she would not harm herself, the room, or me. When she was able to make artwork or have a therapeutic conversation about her home life, she focused on how wrong it was to hit someone. I became enamoured with this young girl because of her adamant denouncement of the violence that she had to endure. I saw her as a little freedom fighter, and revelled in her outright rebellion. She allowed me to show some of her artwork to her mother, who then began to understand the impact that the violence was having on her children. Within a week of seeing her daughter's artwork, the mother left the abusive household with her daughter. Because of the move, I did not see the family again. I am hopeful that the little girl understands the role her rebellion played in saving her family from further violence.

Being known

Children need their caregivers to lovingly witness their strengths, weaknesses, interests and qualities. This allows children to start creating an informed, moral and empowered identity.

While facilitating a learning experience for an anti-violence group for teens, I was able to witness the role that the arts can play in giving voice to each individual in a large group. The structure of the anti-violence group provided each youth with the opportunity to learn many different visual, linguistic and performance art media. After these lessons, the youth could decide to create a piece of art that would be compiled into a group performance.

As in most groups, there were a few youth who quietly resisted engaging in group activities, and could not find a medium they felt comfortable with. As facilitators, our strategy was to designate a worker to care for each of these quiet individuals. I began checking in with an aboriginal youth who regularly chose to work on a painting in a corner, separate from the others. After several weeks, he approached me when others in the group were asking for help with a new art piece. He wanted to write a traditional drumming song about persevering in the face of racism. He refused to work on it with the other people in the room, despite the fact that most of the process involved silently writing the lyrics on paper. I thought of this process as being similar to a teen needing to go a fishing trip with his parent without his siblings. During group hours, we worked in a separate room on his lyrics and drum beats; after group, he went home to practise the performance. I'm happy to say that, at the end of term performance, he stood on stage by himself and performed the song in front of over 200 people.

Key points

Rebecca's stories show how teachers and caregivers can:

1. assume responsibility for the relationship and for cultivating and preserving the connection with children;

2. introduce creative and responsive processes in which adults take the initiative in providing contact and closeness;

3. take responsibility for the process of connecting with children as they guide them for six or more hours during the school day.

3. Taking the lead as adults in a child's life

We must make it easy for our children to connect with us, and look for ways to run to, rather than away from, them.

—Bev Ogilvie

Adults in school communities must prioritize relationships and create a safe haven for children by making them feel welcome and by standing up for them. This means putting the needs of our children before our own and assuming the caretaker role.

All too often, I discover children in our classrooms, homes and communities who report that they live in loveless voids where their basic developmental needs are not met and they are not special to anyone. Many do not feel safe being nurtured by adults, so they strive to be in the lead, on top, the boss. Sadly, for them, it is never enough. They are never free of the pursuit of closeness and they are continuously foraging for love and approval. Very simply, their attachment needs are not being met.

To take the lead is to take care of the child and assume complete responsibility for the relationship, leaving nothing to chance. It means being mindful of the following:

1. Children are creatures of attachment who are meant to depend on those responsible for them.

2. Necessary for growth and development, attachment is primarily intended to facilitate caretaking of the immature. Just as the child must be attached to the parent in order for the parent to do his/her job effectively, it is the nurturing

relationship between the child and the educator that creates the possibility for learning to take place.

3. A child's attachment provides the adult with the natural authority to:

   a. create hierarchy, take charge of them, care for them;

   b. tolerate them, assume responsibility for them, feel compassion and generosity towards them;

   c. create a sense of home, connection and belonging;

   d. provide comfort, nurturing, rest and a place of retreat;

   e. be a compass point, guiding and directing them;

   f. get their attention, secure their cooperation and manage them; and

   g. activate proximity (closeness) instincts in the child.

4. Children spontaneously attach with adults if the qualities and conditions in our classrooms, homes and communities are right. Caring is spontaneous when children are dependent on adults who assume a healthy responsibility for the relationship.

5. Children want to be near, to be the same as, to matter and feel important to, and to be appreciated and cherished by, the adults to whom they are connected. Children try to keep our favour by copying our mannerisms, words, values and beliefs.

6. Vulnerability is at the core of all emotions and feelings. It is the birthplace of love, belonging, hope, joy, courage, empathy and creativity.

7. Many children appear to have lost their vulnerable feelings. They are emotionally hardened, shut down, detached or closed off. They may show a tough exterior, with little or no fear, and seem incapable of being hurt. There is a huge cost to this invulnerability. There is a loss of the ability to function optimally in stressful situations, and there is a numbing of

emotions, a loss of empathy and caring. This leads to social, emotional and behavioural problems in schools, such as aggression, problematic substance use, addictions, boredom and bullying.

So what can we adults do about this loss of vulnerable feelings in many of our children?

As children face more wounding, it is vital that we shield their hearts. It is important that we soften children's hearts so they can get their feelings back. Simply sitting with them and listening with an open heart is a protective practice and a healing connection.

We must get back in the driver's seat, to soften children's defences so as to allow them to find rest and more easily move towards being taken care of. Adults can support resilience by acting as a comforter and by promoting adaptive functioning.

It is imperative that we raise children who believe in their worthiness, which means letting our facial expressions show that we are glad to see them, to be with them, when they walk into the room. These first looks are 'worthiness builders'.[7] Cultivating worthiness in children means making sure they know that they belong and that their belonging is unconditional.

The challenge of becoming a gracious educator (or parent, for that matter) is to not make a child's sense of significance conditional upon certain expectations being met. Rather, it is to convey to the child, in the context of any shortcoming, his/her unconditional significance. There is such power in conveying to the child that he/she is significant even if he/she did not score a goal in the hockey game! Conveying to a child that he/she is 'enough' will help him/her to take off the mask and the armour. With this sense of being enough comes an embrace of worthiness, boundaries and engagement.

---

7   Brown, 2012, p224

As educators, we can get lost in a child's behaviours and feel overwhelmed by them. We can get bogged down in details, strategies and programs. We may feel disillusioned by the challenges of the job, isolated and alone. We might find ourselves searching for answers.

The answers very simply lie in our belief that we are a child's best bet, in knowing that we, the adults (not the child), are in charge of the relationship. It means working at the connection and letting the connection work *for* us.

The key to seizing the lead is in believing that the adult *is* the answer, not that the adult *has* the answer. It is about tapping into an inner well of generosity and grace, and reaching the hearts of children before attempting to teach them. **It is reacting less and relating more. It is connecting more and correcting less.**

Key points

1. Being emotionally connected is a fundamental need for every human being.

2. Caring for children and taking the lead (creating what Neufeld calls "soft hearts and right relationships") are essential conditions for children's attachment to us. We must 'reach before we can teach'.

3. Our task is to deliberately and mindfully increase the number and quality of relationships in the lives of children and families.

4. We must remind ourselves that adaptation is an emotional process and that resilience develops as futility is encountered and felt.

The following stories showcase how teachers and support staff, while focusing on keeping their hearts soft and what it means to be in right relationship with children, have purposefully and intentionally taken the lead.

Educational assistants leading the way

by Sarah Coleborn and Troy Closs

A school store, run by the students of our inner-city elementary school, affords us the opportunity as educational assistants to forge bonds with at-risk students, to have them anchor with us, grow and develop, discover new skills and explore values. Our school motto, 'Safe, Welcome and Comfortable', guides us in making the decision to have the store run by our most vulnerable students who struggle with a sense of belonging. The store creates an environment for positive interactions for the crew (children working in the store) with staff members and the many other students purchasing food. Each crew member has a defined role and is placed in a situation where mutual cooperation is needed in order for the store to run successfully. A community business supports us by donating popcorn. The staff is supportive and accommodating. A resource teacher has joined the team and assists with coordination. The Parent Advisory Council (PAC) has donated money for us to buy a theatre-style popcorn-maker. Each week, the money the store earns is given to our school secretary, who deposits it into an account. The money is then used to support our community in accessing opportunities, thereby becoming another tool for reaching out and connecting with kids.

Community access is a fabulous tool for building attachments and delivering a functional curriculum. It is delivered in its natural setting to those students who are most in need of learning basic functional skills. Community access includes activities such as swimming, skating, using public transit, and tours of interesting places such as a bakery, a recycling depot and the local fire station. We include our students with special needs, our students who are at risk, and some positive peer role models.

A community outing or 'attachment ritual' takes place every Friday morning at our school. We gather at the front doors of our school and then, as an excited, happy group, walk to our local community gathering place—the neighbourhood coffee shop. Numerous staff members, teachers, the school counsellor, speech and language pathologist and our custodian, to name a few, order specialty teas or coffees for students to bring back to them. Students help take the order and the money and off we go. Connections are made between our students with special needs and other students with whom they might not otherwise interact. We address traffic safety issues and familiarize our students with community landmarks and businesses. We often pop into the local business that donates popcorn to our school store. Familiar faces at the business see familiar faces from our school. Community connections are made, which are vitally important to our students with disabilities. For some students, it is a surreal experience sitting with school staff in a coffee shop. For our special needs students, it is a wonderful, inclusive experience. For all of us, there is a sense of connection. Upon our return to school, the students deliver the refreshment orders to the staff. The staff enjoy receiving their tea or coffee as well as the opportunity to positively interact with a student. This non-academic experience lays the groundwork for success in the classroom.

The talent show hinges on students working together as a cohesive team and the successful inclusion of all grades (from kindergarten up to Grade 7) and abilities. Our primary focus, while in the lead ourselves, is to encourage students to become 'upstanders', not bystanders. We look for strengths and attributes. Adults place students in positions where they are most likely to succeed. For example, a student who is proficient with computers would be placed on a team in charge of producing a Power Point presentation for the end of the show. A student who may be technically inclined would be in charge of lighting or audio for the production.

Over the years, participation has increased as more and more students want to be a part of a production that teachers, parents, family members and peers will see. In Year 4, over 150 students from our school were involved. Everyone who participates, no matter what their role, gets a certificate of participation. Having students be part of a team challenges them, makes them accountable to their teammates, and helps them to feel significant. Success is not measured by cheers but by the relationships forged and lessons learned. Former students, who have moved on to high school, often come back to visit, particularly around the time the talent show is being produced, because they still feel a strong connection. In early September, we start getting questions about the show and when it will be held. Some students start work on their creative endeavour for the show early in the school year, even though the show is held in May or June.

The talent show showcases our deep attachments with children. These attachments have made our jobs fulfilling, exciting and challenging. Each day, work for us is sheer joy, made all the more rewarding because we make a difference in children's lives.

Lunchtime intramurals have become one of our most effective ways of forging attachments with children. Intramurals allow us to connect with children, while providing a safe, welcome and comfortable arena. They also serve as motivation for otherwise unmotivated students to go to school. On Mondays and Fridays, anyone (from at-risk students and students with different abilities, to our kindergartens) is welcomed to join us in the gym. However, involvement does come with some behavioural and academic stipulations. All students are held accountable by their individual classroom teachers and supervising staff. This chain of accountability resonates throughout the school. It is a common occurrence at our school to hear older children prompting their younger friends and teammates to make better choices. These prompts often come from students who may have difficulty making their own choices.

Our **Primary Games** have ranged from soccer, hockey, baseball and football to yoga. This forum also allows students to find, explore and develop leadership skills, thus becoming more positive and proactive role models for our community. Once we have our students wanting to attend school, we, in turn, create more enthusiastic learners. A happy student is an easier student to teach!

Key points

1. It is essential that adults prioritize being in the lead with children, to purposefully and intentionally connect with them.

2. It is imperative for students and adults to work together as partners in making their school a better place.

3. Improving the learning environment for all students and staff extends far beyond the lesson plan; it involves establishing trusting relationships with all members of the school community.

4. Achieving our human potential

We are because we belong.
—**Desmond Tutu**

What is the key to achieving one's human potential as a civilized, considerate and caring member of society? According to behaviour theory, one must be taught how to be civilized, caring and considerate. Children must be moulded and sculpted into 'well-behaved citizens'.

I, however, see it more broadly. I believe we can all fulfill our human potential and, when provided with a nurturing environment, that potential naturally emerges from within. The work, then, lies in providing an environment that is conducive to the growth and true maturation of children, while removing any impediments to healthy development.

Growth is the result of three kinds of life processes: **adaptive** (having the resilience to handle adversity), **emergent** (having the ability to function independently), and **integrative** (being social and able to simultaneously mix togetherness and separateness). A resilient or adaptive person is made, not born. He/she evolves as a result of coming to terms with the things in life that he/she cannot change or control. In this process, the child learns from his/her mistakes and benefits from failure. Children become resilient as a result of the patterns of stress and nurturing that they experience early in life. Moderate, predictable activation of our brain's stress response system makes for a stronger, flexible and resilient stress response capacity.[8] Unfortunately, predictable, prolonged and extremely stressful experiences profoundly mark the lives of many of our children, carrying through into adolescence and adulthood.

---

8   Perry and Szalavitz, 2006, pp41-42

Emergence and integration are important life processes in a child's development. An emergent child is viable as a separate being. This life process gives rise to a sense of responsibility, curiosity, interest, boundaries, and respect for others. To become a social being involves integration—becoming capable of mixed feelings and conflicting impulses, of self-control and consideration of another person's agenda.

As we mature, we develop the ability to mix different perceptions, senses, thoughts, feelings and impulses simultaneously in the prefrontal cortex, which has a tremendous tempering, regulating and civilizing effect on personality and behaviour.

The process of maturation is influenced by genetics, instruction and socializing. Research shows that a number of genetically influenced factors, such as temperament and intelligence, do significantly contribute to the process. Another factor is the timing of developmental trauma (a type of stressful event that usually occurs repeatedly and cumulatively over a period of time and within specific relationships): the earlier it starts, the more difficult it is to treat and the greater the damage is likely to be.

The most influential factor is the social environment in which the child is raised. Having supportive social networks is vital for both the child and the guardian. As it is said, it does take a village to raise a child! Educating adults about appropriate parenting and early childhood development is therefore critical, and there is much we can do to enhance caregiving and our social environment.[9]

---

9   Ibid

Tackling the issues

We have taken a wrong turn in today's conventional education system. To get back on track, it is vital that educators:

1. look beyond problematic behaviour or a diagnosed disorder to the emotional roots of behaviour;

2. be mindful that many children become emotionally armoured, due to their lives being filled with chaos, neglect and/or violence;

3. understand the role the human brain plays in protecting against feelings that are too overwhelming; and

4. focus on developing qualities and creating conditions that contribute to a sense of belonging and connectedness, while promoting positive mental health.

Key points

- The education system continues to be wrongly preoccupied with consequences and cognition. It almost entirely ignores children's emotional and physical needs.

- Disconnectedness is at the root of many learning and behavioural problems experienced in schools: non-compliance, aggression, under-achievement, and disruptive or impulsive behaviour.

- The answers to the ongoing dilemma of disconnectedness do not lie solely in roles, practices, curricula or programs. They also lie in the context of relationship—in connection.

- The pivotal factor in healthy maturation is human connection.

- Trauma-informed practice enables educators to shift from focusing on what is wrong with the child to focusing on what happened to the child.

- The brain has an instinctive protective mechanism that involves emotional and perceptual filters designed to screen out wounding and painful information. When these protective mechanisms become chronic and pervasive, a state of defensiveness against vulnerability results, thereby impeding maturation.

- The degree to which we protect ourselves from being vulnerable is a measure of our fear and disconnection.[10]

A recent story by my colleague Lis Kroeker speaks to the power of relationship, of adults in the lead, and adaptive functioning in the work that she does with children.

Finding his tears
by Lis Kroeker

This is the story of Jeremy who came to our school to join our Grade 7 class.

The first time Jeremy came into my office, he had been sent to my room to talk about a fight that he had been involved in. Jeremy was to talk to me, the school counsellor, about what had happened, but he was not in a place where he was going to tell me anything. He hid under his hood and shrugged his shoulders when I said or asked him anything.

Unsure of how to get him to open up, I looked at my shelves and noticed a game of Jenga blocks that has been travelling with me since I started counselling. I took them down. As we played, Jeremy took his hood off and started to talk about what had happened in the playground. We talked about how he had reached his frustration point, which had caused him to attack. This was

---

10   Brown, 2010, p2

the delicate beginning of a connection whereby Jeremy started to orient himself to the adults in his life and take their signs and cues. Seven months later, Jeremy is a different person. He has not been involved in violent instances. He comes to the school and immediately heads to the office, where he greets our secretary. Jeremy likes to call her grandma and often goes to her when things start to agitate him. Jeremy has also experienced a caring connection with his classroom teacher. Shannon has involved Jeremy in a number of meaningful jobs around her classroom, which have required Jeremy to come into the building before school, during recess and often after school.

The second check, after signing in with his teacher, is Jeremy's resource teacher, Gerry. Jeremy visits the resource room several times a day, just checking in, making sure that Gerry knows that he is there. He doesn't talk too much with Gerry, but loves to see him and help him out. Jeremy has also connected with our aboriginal worker. While Jeremy does not have an aboriginal background, he loves to bask in her stories of her childhood, her words of wisdom and encouragement, and her gentle way of taking him in as if he were part of her own family.

Jeremy has also created a warm relationship with me, spending most of his recesses in my office, playing, chatting and making jewelry (yes, the act of creating beautiful pieces of jewelry for the girls has been a great discovery for him). He has not fostered many connections with his peers, and we have not insisted on this. He has a village of attachments in our school building, connecting to a number of adults who daily orient him and act as his compass as he navigates through his often difficult and conflict-ridden life.

Recently, Jeremy came looking for me. He was agitated and insisted that we talk. I wasn't sure if this was just a regular quick check-in before he headed to his room, so I invited him in and asked him what was up. I knew from his file, and from my conversations with his mom, that his was a story full of sadness, violence, abandonment and profound loss. And, even though Jeremy was openly connecting with all of us, Jeremy had never talked about any of this with any of us. His story was his secret.

He sat in my room and started to talk about his family, his yearnings, his fears and his story. He started to shake and suddenly started to sob. At first, he tried to cover up his tears by hiding his face with his arms, but he soon allowed his face to be exposed as he continued to talk about his yearnings, his dreams and what he needed to enable him to move on.

He was not the only one with tears. We sat in my office and cried, talked and pondered and, for the first time I felt like there had been some real release for him. After our session, Jeremy went back to class. Though I had told him to be gentle with himself because he had just done some real hard work in my room, he proceeded to engage in his learning like he hadn't done all year. He read and he completed his assignments, he worked on his math and completed his science. He even shared ideas in his class discussions, and apparently even smiled at his peers.

Jeremy appears much lighter since that experience and, although we are not pretending that he will not encounter any more hurdles, he is now in a place where he has been able to find his tears and, through this, has been able to move on to adaptation. Jeremy has moved on with his development.

Key points

1. The adults at Jeremy's school stepped up and stepped in!

2. They rallied to greet him each day, to show unconditional positive regard, and to respect and value him.

3. Their caring ways enabled him to feel his vulnerability, shed his armour, and move from mad to sad.

4. It was not a program or curriculum that changed him; it was people who changed him!

5. Preventing or intervening in challenging behaviour

Enable me to reach with wisdom,
for I help to shape the mind.
Equip me to teach with truth,
for I help to shape the conscience.
Encourage me to teach with vision,
for I help to shape the future.
Empower me to teach with love
for I help to shape the world.
—author unknown

As a certified crisis intervention instructor, I find myself viewing the issue of crisis prevention through the lens of connectedness. Consequently, a number of critical questions come to mind when preventing or intervening in challenging behaviour and potentially dangerous situations:

- Do the students trust that the staff member is in the lead?

- Do the students trust that the staff member will look after them?

- Do the students trust that the staff member will do the right thing?

- Do the students trust that the staff member will handle situations in a fair and responsible manner?

When I think about decreasing adversarial interactions between adults and the children in their charge, I realize that much of what is practised in the education system comes from a 'deficit' approach, meaning that

45

only what the child cannot do is considered. I'm also reminded of the importance of the following:

1. Acknowledgement of children's strengths. An educator's job is to assist children in naming, knowing and nurturing their 'spark(s)'. In this context, there are two important questions to be asked: *What does the child bring to the world that makes the world a better place? What is his/her passion?*

2. Having a positive and healthy philosophy about children. Schools have curricula and codes of discipline, but they often do not have a philosophy that explains why a student is 'exploding' or 'imploding' and how to teach him/her the skills he/she needs in order to stop doing so. A philosophy acknowledging the fact that 'children do well if they are able to' can guide and govern our adult responses when a child is not doing well.

3. Having a clear understanding of the true nature of a child's difficulties. Durable, effective interventions evolve as a result of focusing on a child as someone who has skills to learn and problems to solve. Children with social, emotional and behavioural challenges have compromised thinking skills.[11] Behind every challenging behaviour is an unsolved problem or a lagging skill—or both. In children (and in adults), this results in critical delays in the development of skills relating to flexibility and frustration tolerance. This, in turn, can give the impression that the child is being non-compliant, although he/she is not intentionally being so. Believing that the child is refusing to cooperate leads adults down a dead end, in terms of any intervention they may attempt to make. In such a situation, children have trouble shifting from one mindset to another. They may become overwhelmed with frustration and have difficulty applying rational thought until they calm down. It is not surprising that these emotionally challenged children are likely to find social interactions extremely frustrating. The good news is they can be helped to develop more adaptive social skills, to approach the world in a more flexible manner.

---

11   Greene, 2008

4. Providing children with opportunities for social and emotional learning. When stuck in the midst of frustration, children have 'brain lock'. Dr Daniel Goleman refers to this as "neural hijacking".[12] Ross Greene looks at specific cognitive skills that children need to be trained in, so they are more able to manage explosions of frustration. These include executive skills, language processing skills, emotion regulation skills, cognitive flexibility skills and social skills. It is important to understand that adults must provide opportunities for problems to be solved and skills to be learned and practised. Many Social and Emotional Learning Programs (SEL), such as Roots of Empathy, Paths, and Mind Up, address these skills, which must be rehearsed thoroughly, many times, in order for them to be effective.

5. Encouraging the formation of a community of learners, wherein a social curriculum is emphasized as much as the academic curriculum. Here, teachers act as role models. They provide frequent opportunities for children to engage in cooperative learning, to practise social interactions and to help each other. This includes diversity and cultural programs, mixed grade groupings, peer support, and mentoring programs such as tutoring and mediation, as well as student internships within the school community. One of the most rewarding experiences for me as a high-school counsellor was facilitating the 7-11 program. This involved pairing Grade 11 students with Grade 7 students to assist the latter in the transition from elementary school to high school.

6. Harnessing the power of relationships. It is important to be purposeful and intentional about connecting children to adults, and to ask the following questions: *What are we doing to connect with children? Are schools linking people on a common journey back to the basics, to what is important, to our humanity and our hearts?* This journey promotes relationship-building processes and connecting children to adults. It places strong emphasis on adult-child problem-solving as the primary mechanism for teaching thinking skills, strengthening skills that may be lagging, and for helping children solve problems.

---

12   Goleman, 1996

7. Understanding that children are wired to cooperate. Children respond to being understood and to collaborative approaches—regardless of age. Inviting children to collaborate in problem-solving enables adults to ensure that their concerns about a child's challenges are being addressed and that they are setting appropriate limits to deal with behavioural issues. More importantly, this involvement ensures that adults are equally committed to addressing children's concerns. The adult, who is in the role of a 'surrogate frontal lobe' or the 'tour guide' through the child's frustration, effectively invites the child to solve the problem with him or her.

I see this lack of invitation to the child to problem-solve as the main difference between collaborative problem-solving approaches and positive behaviour support (PBS). Even though both approaches are proactive and preventative interventions, and both are founded in the belief that children with challenging behaviours should be treated with the same level of interest and importance as children with academic challenges, PBS does not adequately emphasize collaboration between adult and child. PBS is primarily adult-driven and emphasis is placed on adult concerns. Less emphasis is placed on enlisting the child in action plans. Adults come up with the action plan unilaterally and little attention is given to the relationship or to the qualities and conditions that lead to positive mental health.

Collaborative problem-solving is a dramatic departure from the view that challenging kids are attention-seeking, manipulative, coercive and poorly motivated. The approach sets forth the tenet that what is getting in the way of behaviourally challenging children is best understood as the result of cognitive skills that children lack, such as language processing and problem-solving, rather than as the result of passive, permissive, inconsistent parenting. Knowing what skills the child is lacking enables the adult to identify the unsolved problem the child is having difficulty with and to meet the child's needs.

Inviting the child to collaboratively problem-solve lets the child know that the solution to the problem is not predetermined and that solving the problem is something the adult is doing *with* him/her, rather than *to* him/her. In this way, children are held accountable through their participation in a process that they identify with and that articulates their concerns or perspectives, while taking into account those of the adult. This non-punitive, non-adversarial approach, which has the adult in problem-solving mode rather than behaviour-modification mode, compassionately and productively engages the child in a discussion in which the problem or unmet expectation is resolved in a mutually satisfactory manner. Rather than imposing adult will and intensive use of reward and punishment procedures, the best way to reduce challenging episodes is working together with the child as problem-solving teammates. The collaborative approach opens up the lines of communication, allows for realistic goal achievement and facilitates the reduction of challenging behaviour in a mutually satisfactory and durable fashion. It teaches skills the child is lacking, while creating a supportive relationship.

Key points:

1. All children have an inborn need to seek an all-powerful 'other' to provide a sense of security and belonging and to be a source of values.

2. Many children are not anchored with caring adults. They are morally and spiritually adrift, lured by superficial connections to each other that can often leave them feeling empty, angry, depressed and self-destructive.

3. It is important for educators, who are called upon most frequently to help when problems occur, to have a basic understanding of collaborative problem-solving, primary principles of positive behaviour support and attachment-based strategies.

4. Educators are encouraged to be authoritative but not authoritarian—controlling learning environments but not the child. A progressive learning culture values all learners. It embraces relevant and current curricula as well as instruction

and assessment practices that are tailored to individual interests, needs and backgrounds.

5. It is vital that educators draw on experiences, mechanisms and processes to cultivate empathy and a genuinely generous spirit in youth. Fostering empathy in children can help them thrive emotionally, physically and academically.

6. SEL programs provide children with the tools to help them understand their own emotions, respond to stress, focus quietly, build confidence and improve academic performance.

7. It is essential that educators weave compassion and responsibility into the fabric of the curriculum. A logical place to begin is to give children and youth opportunities to develop caring behaviour that extends beyond their circle of friends.

8. Make schools not only places to learn but also healthy, cohesive communities.

9. Build partnerships with the faith community, local businesses and agencies, the police, mental health institutions, and juvenile justice to provide a community-wide network of support for students at risk. Encourage those providing services and support to work directly with the school.

10. Provide consistent and ongoing opportunities for authentic participation of parents and students.

The following story illustrates that, when trust is lacking, student achievements suffer and dysfunction escalates. It also demonstrates that student aggression decreases when schools build a culture of calmness, collaborative problem-solving and connectedness. Best practices in our schools and communities rest on a staff attitude of helpfulness, respect and support. Many crises can be prevented if these pieces are in place and if our first priority is to build connection, wherever possible.

Sandy's story
by Fran De Tracie

Sandy is a poor child whose mother is a drug addict. Her aunt received custody of Sandy when Sandy was very little. Sandy struggles academically but has never been properly psycho-educationally tested. She is regularly victimized by her classmates, and her teacher struggles to address the issue. There has been some intervention by the school counsellor but she is only there part time. Sandy receives some academic support from an Educational Assistant (EA) whose caseload is very heavy, but who does her best to mentor her with some emotional support.

Sandy attempts to deal with the class bullies by threatening them with her older cousins, with whom she lives. Nothing is actually resolved because Sandy and her needs are somewhat invisible at home. Her aunt does not attend school concerts, sports day, or parent–teacher conferences. Sandy never has any money for special lunches and is poorly dressed in second-hand clothes.

This year, a spot for Sandy has opened up with me—the school custodian. I save certain fix-it jobs for Sandy around the school, which we do at lunchtime for about a half-hour. For instance, the doll's crib in kindergarten broke and we worked on that for a few sessions. Later, we worked on a chart stand to be constructed for a teacher.

Sandy loves this kind of activity and is very confident with tools, even if she doesn't know how to use them. She has watched her cousins fixing cars and other things, and has a strong belief that she can figure things out. I allow her to take all the time she needs on these projects. After all, there is no rush and the real point of my time with her is to support her in feeling good about herself.

Between the counsellor, the EA and myself, we are helping Sandy to cope. We give her leadership responsibility for the primary students and this helps, too, because she sees herself as mature and capable.

Once a year, I bring my mounted hawks in and do a 'Hawk Talk' in each classroom. Sandy is my assistant when I do this. We start off in the least intimidating setting—in kindergarten. As Sandy learns the details, she takes on more and more of the talks so that, by the time we arrive at her class, she is introduced as a 'hawk expert'. Because we have set her up in the right way, she is able to play this role. This helps her classmates to see her differently. True support means all pulling together to help the kids, and not letting 'job descriptions' get in the way.

In this scenario, Fran did a number of very powerful things for Sandy. She:

1. invited Sandy to exist in her presence;

2. encouraged her, while recognizing and nurturing her sparks;

3. mentored her;

4. acknowledged her significance to her peers; and

5. cultivated (through what they shared in common) a deep relationship with Sandy, which enabled her to feel safe, that she belonged and that she mattered.

6. Understanding crisis development

Teaching compassion in schools goes a long way.
—**Craig and Marc Kielburger**

As an instructor with the Crisis Prevention Institute (CPI), I teach the Crisis Development Model—a program focused on the safe management of disruptive and assaultive behaviour. This model has four clear stages of crisis development (behaviour levels), with corresponding staff attitudes and approaches (see table below). From the CPI's perspective, it is essential that staff respond at all levels with compassion and with the intention of promoting the care, safety, welfare and security of those being cared for. The table below illustrates the CPI model from a crisis development/management perspective.

Behaviour level	Staff attitude/approach
A. Anxiety	Show empathy, support
B. Defensiveness	Be directive, set limits
C. Physically acting out	Use non-violent physical crisis intervention
D. Tension reduction	Therapeutic rapport

A. A crisis begins with a child presenting as anxious. The appropriate staff response is to alleviate this anxiety through empathic responses and by being supportive.

B. The crisis may escalate, however, to the next level of defensiveness or non-compliance, whereby the child is saying "no" and is demonstrating dissatisfaction with the situation. When the child is being defensive, his/her auditory channels are shutting down and the way to take control of this situation is to be directive and set limits. In this stage, which is still verbal, staff are encouraged to resist power struggles, to let the child vent, if possible, to remove the audience and to rely on team support if the child becomes verbally intimidating.

C. The third stage sees the child physically out of control and a risk to self and others. As a last resort, staff may decide to use least-restrictive and least-intrusive, safe, non-harmful control and restraint techniques.

D. Finally, in the fourth stage, the child cannot maintain a high level of energy so, ultimately, he/she returns to a state of compliance and tension reduction. Staff are expected to focus on therapeutic rapport and rebuilding the relationship.

Crisis development: a connectedness model

What might a crisis development model look like in the context of connectedness? The following table illustrates a typical progression. It starts with the child not feeling at a place of rest, then moving through the alarm and agitation stages before returning to rest. Staff responses are focused on relationship, not behaviour.

Behaviour level	Staff attitude/approach
A. Unrest	Connect, attend to, show interest in, the child; create an environment of trust and compassion; act as child's compass point/guide.
B. Alarm	Focus less on behaviour, more on context of relationship; alter situations and circumstances that trigger problem behaviour.
C. Agitation (fight or flight or freeze)	Focus on safety; shield from threat.
D. Calm and rest	Focus on restoring the relationship with the child; foster awareness of what alarms the child—i.e., frustration, pursuit, fear.

Regardless of the model you embrace, it is critical that you understand that, under severe stress, everyone becomes less rational, less empathic, and more impulsive. The more distressed we become, the less active our higher, more considerate regions of the brain become. Threat pushes us to rely on lower, more primitive regions of the brain. Our level of arousal—from calmness, slight apprehension and fear to all-out panic—affects our ability to make good choices. "Understanding this arousal continuum reveals a lot about how the world works. If we want a kinder, more caring society, people need more experiences and places in which they feel safe. If we want to be kind to others or have others respond with empathy toward us, we need to minimize unpredictable and highly tense situations and maximize our ability to deal with ordinary stress."[13]

Understanding that persistent stress alters the biology of the brain and body makes it even clearer why we are seeing an increase in the incidence of mental illness in our schools. High levels of chronic stress that starts in early life doesn't just cause physical illness. It increases the risk of virtually every known form of mental illness, including depression, bipolar disorder, schizophrenia, addiction, and post-traumatic stress disorder.

The good news is there is an antidote to uncontrollable stress: the kindness of others. Stress is modulated by positive social contact. To remove children's stress, we simply need to be a loving presence—respectful, patient and understanding. The best formula for recovery from a traumatic experience is founded on stable, safe relationships.

I am often asked in my role as district counsellor how to educate the hearts of children. The answer, in a nutshell, is to develop the universal values of altruism, compassion and connectedness in children. It is crucial that we teach kids not only how to read but also how to relate. We need to encourage compassionate action and create conditions and emotional states conducive to it. It is also important to teach empathy because it is the foundation of pro-social behaviour. It produces kindness and calmness, both of which create safety.

Developing compassion starts with you, the teacher, in your classroom. Your attitude, in particular, and the words you choose can determine

---

13   Perry, 2010, pp198-199

the outcome of an interaction, and escalate or de-escalate the situation. As Pearl Strachan says: "Handle them carefully for words have more power than the atom bomb."[14]

Words carry more than their literal meaning. They can communicate hope, possibility and optimism. They can communicate positive emotions such as gratitude, increase happiness and help children learn and remember things better.

Kind words nurture feelings of gratitude and joy. They have the ability to forge a caring community and to change the culture of our schools. For example, think of the difference between 'sit down', and 'would you please take a seat'. Which one evokes care, welfare, safety and security? Which one encourages a power struggle?

Words have particular power when we are setting limits. 'It is time to clean your room' is very different from 'Would you like to clean your room before or after lunch?' The latter empowers the individual; the former takes power away. Also, paraverbals—the volume, tone and cadence (rhythm) of our words—have a big influence on the outcome. We have all found ourselves in situations where we've increased a child's alarm (and that of ourselves and others too!) by raising our voice or by having a condescending tone.

Essentially, in order to prevent crises (and build ConnectZones), these basic questions must be addressed:

- Are we creating an environment of connection, trust and compassion?

- Are we promoting tolerance and inclusion in our classrooms/ schools? Or is there an illusion of inclusion?

- Are we using collaborative process to develop classroom agreements and rules of conduct? Are we involving students and parents in reviewing/rewriting school policies?

---

14   Schill, 2010

- Are we placing more emphasis on collaboration and less on competition?

- Are we educating hearts and minds?

- Are we helping others and giving back to the world?

- Are we relating well to each other, taking an interpersonal perspective?

- Are we avoiding words that create a negative emotional response?

- Are we precipitating heightened emotions that trigger crisis situations?

- Are we reading the child's behaviour, rather than reacting to it?

- Are we seeing the child, not just the behaviour?

- Are we setting limits with the intention of educating the child and helping him/her feel safe and secure?

- Are we providing guidance and being respectful, or are we setting punitive limits to show who is boss?

- Are we on a mission to crush the child (or the parent or even a colleague) under the weight of authority, to control, coerce, dominate or win?

- Are we rigid and reactive?

- Are we building bridges or putting up fences?

The following story is about the essential role that prevention plays in classroom management. It highlights the power of a loving, caring adult presence, as well as the importance of developing positive relationships, trust and rapport in reaching challenging kids. I'm reminded of the power of empathy with children—how it allows them to stay calm and to solve problems. Empathy helps to de-escalate tension in the child and increase the chance of resolution. It allows us to achieve the best possible understanding of a child's concern or perspective.

The teacher 'rocked' and captivated me

by Lis Kroeker

The room was full of noise; students chatting and shuffling chairs as they prepared themselves for their science class; laughter, paper airplanes flying across the room. And then the door opened. The room went still and the students stood up, watching intently as their teacher, Herr Büehlman, came into the class.

We were visiting his class 25 years after we had been there as his students. We sat at the back of the room. I cast my mind back to when Herr Büehlman was my teacher. I must have been 14 or 15 at the time. My teenage hormones were raging—leading me through moods of highs and lows. I was filled with wonder, living from moment to moment, not always able to connect to all that was happening to me at the time. And I was a dreamer. I often forgot my work, misplaced it, or did not recall ever getting it because I had been dreaming about something else when instructions were given out.

I remember Herr Büehlman asking me to stay behind after class one day, and the fear that came over me because I knew that I wasn't keeping up. When everyone had left the room, he confirmed that I wasn't keeping up, but that he wanted me to be successful. And then he told me his plan. My job that night was to organize my messy papers so I could get started on my work. I was to organize my papers into three categories: ones that were completed and made sense to me, ones that made no sense to me, and a list of papers that I found confusing. The next day, I stayed after school and we went through my piles of paper. Then he told me to come back every day after school, with some of these sheets completed and with questions. We did this until I understood a question. Then he allowed me to go home.

I don't remember threats. I don't even know if he made the ominous call to my parents indicating I wasn't getting my work done. I remember his caring. I remember his determination to see me pass his course. And I remember that it was in his class that I discovered that I was able to be a successful learner. His class was a turning point for me. He showed me that I could do this, and he believed that I could.

Twenty-five years later, now a teacher myself, I sat in his class as a guest, and got to watch him in action again. After he finished greeting his students, and welcoming them to his class, he asked them to sit down. Then he took a rock from his desk, looked at it inquisitively and said to his students: "We have a problem that we need to solve. Come close and look at this rock and tell me what you see." The students moved closer to him, as did we, and looked and responded to his questions. I was amazed at his craft, at how he could invite these hormone-filled teenagers into what could appear to be a question of no relevance to them. Except that it became relevant because it was his question, and he had invited them to it.

As I watched him teach, I noticed a girl standing back a bit, not really saying too much. And then he stopped, looked at her and said: "Mary, what do you think about this?" He looked at her, smiled, nodded and waited... and she answered.

Key points

1. Both children and adults need continuous encouragement in order to develop and gain a sense of belonging.

2. Encouragement is central. It promotes change and, when communicated with sincerity and belief in the child, reinforces intrinsic motivation, assisting in the development of goals, desirable attitudes, and competence.

7. Understanding a child from the inside out

A person's world is only as big as their heart.
—Tanya A. Moore

Children are meant to depend on adults; they need to rest in our care. If this care is lacking, children will look elsewhere for it, or seek it in each other. If that happens, other behaviours can kick in. They may become bossy or obsessed with winning or getting the best marks. They may dominate in the classroom or the playground—which can be a recipe for disaster. These behaviours may fuel their resistance and frustration, often resulting in acts of desperation. They may lash out or turn their frustration inward in the form of self-harm.

Educators need to be cognisant of the fact that the internal states generated by alarm and threat profoundly affect one's capacity for thought and control over one's behaviour. When calm, we are more creative and productive. Reactions are driven by the cortex and neocortex, allowing us to respond to flexible, nurturing and enriching approaches and even plan for the future. If under direct threat, however, the focus of all problem-solving becomes the immediate present, and solutions are more reactive and regressive.

When children are in a state of high alarm or terror, their attention focuses on what threatens, what is wrong or unsafe and on avoiding harm to their own body. Physiologically, their reactions are driven by lower areas of the brain. "There will be no rational thinking, merely reflexive responses directed to self-preservation. Understanding the arousal continuum (from calmness to slight apprehension to fear and then to all-out panic) can help us understand why people are kinder and more considerate when calm, and less capable of making best choices when stressed."[15]

As educators, we experience children (and adults) who 'tune out', seemingly lacking in caution, concern and caring because they feel unsafe and defensive. They may be facing unbearable separation brought on by death, rejection or attachment loss.[16]

They may be vulnerable to feelings of insignificance or of not mattering, of not being known, of not being liked, or of being too much to handle. They may 'numb out' or 'tune out' due to being excluded, or as a result of a loss of contact, a lack of belonging, an unbearable difference, not fitting in or because they are not being seen. (See Chapter 2 on how children are meant to attach.)

Children can alternate between two states:[17] an alarm state and a dissociative state. An alarm state may be reflected in elevated heart rate and blood pressure, and high activity. In extreme cases, this produces rage, sadness-filled tantrums, and physical manifestations such as climbing on things and hyperactivity. Or there may be primitive dissociative responses to extreme stressors, such as dull, spacey moods, feelings of numbness, depression, lowered heart rate and blood pressure, withdrawal, becoming physically small and distant. This calls to mind children driven by the most primitive systems in the brain stem, who are incapable of, or ineffective at, fighting or fleeing, and who make themselves as small as possible by curling up in a foetal position under a table.

---

15   Perry, 2010, pp338-339
16   Neufeld and Mate, 2005
17   Perry, 2010

Educators are encouraged to be up to speed on the latest brain research, which reveals the following:

1. Relationships shape neural circuits in the brain and impact self-regulation.

2. Secure human attachment promotes flexible self-regulation, pro-social behaviour, empathy, a positive sense of emotional well-being and self-esteem.

3. Many children diagnosed with ADHD are really not disordered but are restless and agitated, unable to sense alarming feelings. THIS DOES NOT IMPLY THAT THEY DO NOT HAVE THESE FEELINGS. Rather, they are simply unable to access them. They are untempered, not moved to caution or to feelings of sadness and disappointment. For them, **knowing better does not lead to behaving better.**

4. Extreme tantrums, sensory problems, difficulties with social interactions and empathy, and repetitive primitive self-soothing behaviours are common to both autism and developmental trauma.

5. Children born into and raised with chaos, threat and trauma have been marinated in fear and are frequently in a hyper-aroused state.

6. Trauma creates an experience of overwhelming helplessness, which compromises our ability to make choices.

7. A lack of a sense of self-efficacy can be a crippling result of trauma, whereby resilience is compromised.

8. Too much stress moves us to alarm, fear or terror, compromising our ability to learn.

9. Children who are calm and alert can take in new information. We all need emotional safety to maximize our learning.

10. Kind social contact relieves distress, reducing the toll of high levels of stress hormones on the body.

Educators know, all too well, that neglected children or those with other attachment disruptions are much harder to soothe and teach. We know from experience that it takes a great deal more attention to calm them down and make them feel better. Often, we are witness to their incredible neediness, their inability to complete schoolwork without clowning around or receiving constant praise and guidance. We experience many children who do not find relationships rewarding, who lack a moral compass, seek thrills in physical pleasures and wield power over others. For them, it can be a dog-eat-dog world—every man for himself.

We can no longer remain unaware of what shapes a child's behaviour or ignore the emotional needs of our children. When children are not in right relationship with adults, their stress is increased, they are filled with anxiety and they are in a state of unrest and alarm—all of which interferes with their ability to learn. The arousal state prompts children to lose control, and to act impulsively and aggressively. These are natural responses... so why punish them? Instead, let's help them in the following ways:

a. Provide stability through routine and predictability.

b. Provide consistency and familiarity.

c. Offer affection and close attention.

d. Nurture physical and emotional closeness.

e. Listen with an empathic, open heart.

f. Pattern repetitive experiences in a safe environment, appropriate to children's developmental needs.

g. Expose them to developmentally appropriate enrichment experiences, such as rocking and being held in a respectful, caring manner.

h. Use music, dance and massage to stimulate lower brain regions that contain key regulatory neurotransmitter systems involved in the stress response.

i. Provide opportunities for them to have a sense of control over who they talk to and what they discuss, and to process at their own pace, in their own ways.

j. Decrease chaos and stress levels in the classroom, as well as sensory overload.

k. Encourage ongoing supportive, stable relationships, including peer relationships.

l. Heal through a nurturing community and a rich social world.

m. Reconnect them with those things that provide a sense of connection, aliveness and safety.

n. Teach them alternative coping skills and promote relaxation in the classroom.

o. Teach them about the brain and that outbursts are often prompted by frustration, a sense of rejection and feeling misunderstood.

p. Promote cross-organizational communication and planning.

It is extremely important for educators to understand that many children grow up with underdeveloped limbic and relational neural systems that limit them to shallow, superficial relationships. This faulty relational neurobiology explains their inability to derive pleasure from healthy human relationships, their lack of interest in people and their lack of empathy. Because their brains are still developing, young children are at great risk of suffering lasting effects of trauma. Lingering terror, especially early in life, may cause an enduring shift to a more impulsive, aggressive, less thoughtful and less compassionate way of responding to the world.

The following story shows how early attachment problems can be mitigated by strong, later-life relationships, reminding us that healthy communities buffer the pain and often prevent interpersonal trauma from happening in the first place. Wade's story is about rebuilding trust, regaining confidence, and having a sense of security and connection. It emphasizes the importance of including children, protecting them and freeing them from anxiety, fear and stress. Creating an atmosphere of safety in a context of predictable relationships brings a child to a place where he/she feels nurtured and fulfilled. (See Appendix 3 for Wade's strategies for building relationships with his students.)

The power of relationship

by Wade Wilson

I began my work in the Bridge Behaviour Program late in the academic year, at the beginning of April. I was covering for a member of staff who was on maternity leave. As I arrived at the school for my three-day orientation alongside the teacher before she left for the year, I recognized a familiar face. It was the mother of a boy I had worked with intensively six years earlier, when I was just beginning as an Educational Assistant. She was in the office because her son had recently been suspended for fighting. He was in Grade 7, but was attending a bridge-to-high-school program because his behaviours were too challenging for the elementary level.

Throughout his schooling, this large athletic boy had had several problems. His aggression, anger and disrespect towards staff and students saw him shuffled around the district programs. Clearly, his foul frustrations were getting the best of him. His mom was overjoyed to see me, especially when she found out I was to be the replacement teacher for her son. Instead of seeing his return to school with dread and anxiety, Luke saw it as an opportunity to reunite with someone he had fond memories of.

Luke began to attend school regularly and settled himself into a routine. There were no further incidents that year and I was fortunate enough to be awarded another contract for the following year, so I was able to continue working closely with Luke. He turned his attitude around and became much less verbally abusive, both at school and at home. He didn't get suspended for any acts of aggression or defiance and he managed, with some assistance, to pass several grade-level courses. He would come to me when he was having difficulty and together we would problem-solve. When he realized I was sticking around and there was no problem or situation we couldn't solve together, he got more involved in school activities. The year passed with him not failing any courses. More importantly, his relationships with family and friends were stronger and healthier than ever before.

The following year, he involved himself in even more activities throughout the school. He joined the basketball, volleyball and soccer teams. He helped keep score, late into the evenings, for visiting school teams. He acquired friends who were doing quite well in their classes, so they helped him with his studies and class work. One friend convinced him to become involved in a school club called SWAT (Students Welcoming All Teens). He went on to play a big part in promoting the Pink Shirt Day (an anti-bullying/anti-homophobia event) and a Stop-the-Violence day. The youth worker in charge wanted to promote Luke to the role of mentor for young kids at elementary schools.

Key points

1. Luke was anchored by a caring adult who believed in the transformative power of relationship.

2. Luke learned that he belonged, that he had something to offer the world and that there were people who cared about him.

The next story similarly portrays connectedness and how it empowers as a comforter—again reminding us that human connection reduces the sense of aloneness and terror that many children experience. It demonstrates the power of being deeply and safely connected to caring adults, which enables children to feel their feelings—especially the tender, vulnerable ones—so they can be moved to caution, rest and growth.

"I am walking home."

by Lis Kroeker

"I am walking home," explained Jonah to Mrs Comer, at the side of the road. "Home?" Mrs Comer said. "Where is your home?" Jonah looked at Mrs Comer, puzzled and annoyed. "You know, my school. I am going home!"

Jonah attended our school from kindergarten until the end of last year in Grade 3. He lived in a foster home with his sister and the two grandchildren of his foster parents. Jonah's story was full of sadness. His birth mom was an addict living on the streets of a big city where he and his sister had been found living in crack houses, often going for days without seeing their mom. No one knew who Jonah's father was. Jonah and his sister were abused and neglected.

Challenged, not only by the neurological damage to his brain as a result of his mom's addictions, but also by his traumatic life situation, Jonah attended our school every day. He connected with his teachers and clung to anyone who made him feel safe. His teacher made Jonah feel welcome in her classroom. She greeted him every morning when he arrived, she cheered him on as he struggled to learn to read and write, and she celebrated his growth as a person.

Often, Jonah became overwhelmed by his surroundings and, as his confusion and alarm rose, his ability to regulate his emotions disappeared. He became violent and attacked those around him. On one of these occasions, Jonah ended up hurting his teacher. He panicked, grabbed her and dug his nails into her arms. Calmly and with amazing courage, the teacher spoke to him softly, assuring him that he was safe and that she wasn't going to leave him. The next day, she stood by the door of the school, ready to welcome him back, and she sat with him in a quiet place to talk about what the day would look like and how they would get through it. Jonah was horrified by the fact that he had hurt her, and she offered him her forgiveness and assurance that she loved him very much.

Late in the school year, the foster parents informed the school that Jonah would be moving to a different foster home. School personnel met with the family and the social worker and pleaded for them to keep Jonah at the school. But it appeared to be beyond the family's control. Jonah said goodbye to us as we closed the school for summer.

Even though Jonah's teacher and our principal visited Jonah's new school in the beginning of the school year to help the new team understand him from the inside out, Jonah was not able to stay in his new school for long. His aggressive behaviour escalated to the point that the new foster family couldn't manage and, by October, Jonah was moved to another foster home and another school. Jonah wanted to come back to our school, but it was against policy, so he was sent to yet another school. By November, Jonah was only able to spend half an hour a day in his new school. He was perceived to be unmanageable and violent. Nobody wanted Jonah. His foster family didn't want him and, again, he was transferred to a new home and a new school. We phoned the school board and told them that we wanted Jonah back in our school, but our requests and offers were not attended to.

It was in the middle of a cold December day that Mrs Comer noticed Jonah walking down the highway and stopped to talk to him. Jonah explained that it would only take five minutes to drive to his new school, but it would take him two hours to walk back home to our school.

Mrs Comer gave Jonah a ride to our school. Our principal chatted with him, hugged him and listened to him, and then had to call the social worker. Jonah was picked up by the social worker and taken away again. This morning, I received a call from the counsellor of the new school that Jonah is to attend. She wanted to know about the safety plan that we had put in place, and wanted me to explain why it was that we hadn't addressed all his aberrant behaviours in our plan.

Our plan was a plan for the adults. It talked about what we would do to help Jonah to feel safe. It talked about how we would manage his environment so that he could be safe. Our safety plan talked about creating a context of connection, where order and structures would be put in place in order to support this child. We talked about a plan that would solicit Jonah's good intentions through our relationship with him. Our safety plan talked about creating a village for him.

I often find myself thinking about Jonah. We were able to give him a place of rest in our school. We gave him a place where he was able to grow and develop and feel safe. I feel overwhelmed by sadness when I think of a little boy walking down a cold road trying to find his way home, and I hope that he'll be able to find it again.

---

8. Soliciting a child's good intentions

Educating the mind without educating the heart is no education at all.

—Aristotle

I recently overheard a conversation between a teacher and a couple of her students about an altercation in the playground. The teacher seemed very agitated and overly preoccupied with a dispute about how many punches had been thrown and how many punches had landed. I thought to myself, *does it really matter?* How frequently in our education system we get caught up in the details!

One of the main principles of safe discipline is ensuring that it is applied in a context of connection. Even with the best intentions, educators often default to bossing children around as a means of imposing order, even though it may go against our deepest intuitions.

As already mentioned, children do well if they are connected to adults, if they have the necessary skills and if adults understand the developmental nature of behaviour. Typically, we insist that children make good choices or face the consequences of not doing so. In reality, however, many children lack the skills and the maturity (adaptive and integrative functionality) to make good choices. Furthermore, the consequences are often ours, not theirs, and there is little or no collaboration with the child about fixing the problem.

Focusing on a child's desire to be good and have good intentions, and on what matters to him/her, definitely has its merits. If a child's intentions are good, then he/she is aiming in the right direction and moving forward. Focusing on the child's good intentions enables us to come alongside the child and mutually trust in our relationship. It draws the child 'on side' and safeguards against contrived methods of control and punishment that erode the relationship. And, finally, it allows us to model and draw out mixed feelings in the child instead of demanding their self-control.

Soliciting a child's good intentions allows him/her to set his/her sights on realistic goals. For example, a child who intends to be safe in the playground will strive to that end. Should he get into a fight, instead of imposing consequences or sanctions, or focusing on the misbehaviour, we can identify with his good intentions rather than his failure. While reminding him that fighting won't work for him, we can, at the same time, be supportive and encouraging, letting him know that we realize he wants to be safe and that we want to help him be safe.

Soliciting children's good intentions allows us to work from a position of influence. We are anticipating problems and acknowledging that we all make mistakes. We need to let children know that they can depend on us; we can take it! In no way are they too much to handle! Their problems are our problems. We are there to help them achieve their intentions and reach their goals.

Seeing a child's good intentions

by Lis Kroeker

Whenever there are issues with children, I find that, if I take the time to explore those issues, there are usually good intentions behind whatever is happening.

In my little country school on Vancouver Island, I was working with a little Grade 1 boy (we shall refer to him as E) who was perceived to be aggressive. In his high alarm, he could lift bookshelves and throw them across the room. Both adults and students in the school were often in high alarm themselves when he was around, concerned that they would not be safe if he became frustrated. I work in a little old portable building at the back of the school. One day, as we were sitting together in my office, working on a puzzle, E smiled at me and said that he was fixing my 'portable'. We giggled and talked about how the portable was falling apart, and he promised me that he would show me later what he was doing. His language is limited, so I must confess that, though curious, I did not have a clear sense of what he meant when he said that he was 'fixing my portable'.

At recess, as I was standing close to the portable, watching kids play, I noticed that E had recruited a number of friends and that they were standing right next to the portable. Upon closer examination, I noticed that they were kicking the skirting boards around the portable and breaking them. I moved closer to see what was happening and, just as E was about to explain, another teacher came running up and started yelling at the boys for destroying school property. I tried to explain to her that I was already looking into this, but she ran into the school building looking for the school principal because she felt that we had an emergency on our hands. I turned back to the boys and asked E what they were doing. He explained that the boards were rotten and needed to be removed so that new ones could be put on (where he was planning on getting new boards from was beyond me). He smiled proudly and told me that he knew what he was doing because he had watched his father fix things in his house many times and this is how he did it. I thanked E and his friends for caring about my portable, and told them that I would let the principal know that it needed to be fixed. Then I sent them off to play for their recess.

The principal came to see what was happening, expecting a crisis. I explained the situation to her and, thankfully, she was able to see behind what appeared to be an act of aggression towards school property. That afternoon, the principal called the carpenter to come and fix the boards, and she invited E to come and help. Now, every time we walk by the portable and reach the spot where the rotten boards were, I see E smiling.

Key points

1. Both Lis and the principal were able to look beyond the behaviour to see the child from the inside out.

2. They saw E's good intention, involved him in the solution, nurtured and championed his spark, and focused on maintaining their relationship with him.

3. They did not use separation to punish him but instead responded in a manner that added to his sense of belonging and significance.

9. Developing education plans to support connectedness

Education plans must indicate that we,
as adults, are a child's place to slow down,
find peace and comfort.

—Bev Ogilvie

The next story relates to adults who are in the lead, acting as compass points for children, and helping them to orient themselves and find their way.

Lynn's story

by Sara Coleborn

Lynn arrived at our inner-city school from a third-world country. She instantly stuck out as a child who was likely to experience problems. In our Grade 1 classroom, where I worked as an EA with two teaching partners, Lynn had a number of eruptions each day, frequently followed by her hiding under a desk, refusing to come out, or running out of the classroom. Lynn had a need for proximity and safety, however, and never went far when she ran off.

Food was a strong connecting tool in building my relationship with Lynn. Upon learning that she frequently did not eat breakfast before school, I took on the responsibility to make sure she had a good breakfast. Each morning, I prepared a glass of water and toast with jam, using bread donated to our school. Her peers wondered, at first, why Lynn was eating toast. Our response was that she was eating to get her brain working for the day. After that, no one asked, and Lynn was no longer engaging in disruptive behaviour or constantly moving on the carpet. By meeting her most basic needs, I hoped to create an environment that was conducive to learning.

When Lynn had trouble managing to stay attentive on the carpet, I would 'collect' her with a gentle voice and a smile, never showing my own feelings of frustration. I sometimes invited Lynn to sit on my lap. She usually accepted this invitation with joy and could sit with me for prolonged periods of time without her typical restlessness.

To me, it is essential that I tell those I'm attempting to foster a relationship with that I care about them. With Lynn, I 'collected' her by greeting her with enormous enthusiasm each morning. This was clearly stated in her Individual Education Plan (IEP). Creating a surrogate 'family' for the class was an IEP goal around which lessons were planned. Providing a home base for Lynn—a caring environment where she could feel safe and at rest—gave me the natural authority to nurture my relationship with her. To help facilitate feelings of compassion in Lynn, I invited her to help me with my primary responsibility—the designated student to whom I was assigned as an educational assistant. Harry, a gentle, passive student who has Autism Spectrum Disorder (ASD), required my support in implementing the curriculum.

Lynn focused her energy on making sure her friend was taken care of. Harry was completely accepting of Lynn and her 'mother hen'-like qualities. We purposely seated Lynn and Harry together during lessons held on the carpet, and during desk work, assemblies and any structured activities where both would likely require support. The positive feedback Lynn received for her kindness and friendship with Harry gave her a sense of success and pride.

There was one teacher in particular with whom Lynn had conflict on a regular basis. This teacher was very generous to Lynn, giving her lots of clothing, as sometimes the clothes Lynn wore were too small for her. The teacher gave her countless pairs of socks as Lynn rarely wore socks, even in the dead of winter. This teacher always made sure that Lynn received plenty of the donated bread to take home to her family. She went out of her way to make sure that Lynn had whatever the school was able to offer.

However, the friction between them continued. It was not unusual to hear Lynn storming out of this teacher's classroom. The teacher acknowledged that the relationship needed some help. I took on the role of matchmaker, with the goal of endearing Lynn to this teacher with whom she had to interact daily. I came to the classes with Lynn and gently scripted how she could respond to any frustrating situations. The teacher allowed Lynn to sit on her lap during the daily routine of doing the calendar, the weather chart etc. She also permitted her to eat a snack during class, as she understood the emotional connection Lynn had with food. I emphasized to Lynn how much the teacher cared about her, as well as pointing out likenesses that they shared.

During our Valentine's Day classroom celebration, I encouraged Lynn to invite this teacher as her special guest so that they could celebrate and enjoy some food together. The teacher rearranged her schedule to be able to attend and it paid off. The connection began to blossom and the teacher was able to move away from using ultimatums and demands. If an incident did arise, the teacher took an approach that would help maintain the relationship. In the event that Lynn looked like her foul frustrations were about to boil over, I would take her out of the classroom for a quiet conversation, to solicit her good intentions and express mixed feelings. This enabled Lynn to recover and return to the classroom with dignity.

As indicated in Lynn's story, Lynn had an IEP that is a concise, usable document developed to support success in a student with special needs. In different places, it may go by a different name, such as Individualized Program Plan, but it similarly describes individualized goals that reflect area(s) of need for the student, adaptations and/or modifications to the regular class program and the support services to be provided. Mechanisms for tracking student growth are also included in the plan.

It is imperative that a collaborative team consisting of classroom teacher(s), the school administrator, other relevant school staff, district support staff, parent(s)/guardian(s) and, where appropriate, the student and members of the community, develop the IEP for the student. (See Appendix 4 for connectedness strategies for IEPs.) This process of collaboration creates the potential to devise a comprehensive plan for the student that is understood and supported by members of this team. The completed plan outlines the learning activities and aspects of the educational program designed to meet the student's unique needs. Goals are broken down into objectives that are specific, measurable, achievable, relevant and timely (SMART). Objectives are defined in terms of observable student learning and identification of skills the child needs, the context regarding where the skills are to be learned, and time frame within which the objectives are to be met. Strategies define the type of skill to be taught and how that will be done, and describe what the person or persons responsible for implementing the strategies will do.

The teacher's role is to assess, adapt or modify certain areas of the curriculum, along with teaching methods, materials and/or evaluation methods, as well as monitor progress. Getting to know students well will facilitate this process. Teachers have, at their fingertips, tools to gather direct evidence of an individual student's self-image and coping strategies, as well as a student's self-understanding and self-advocacy.

It is important to note that the IEP document does not describe every aspect of the student's program. It does, however, refer to those aspects of the educational program that are modified or adapted, and it identifies the support services to be provided. In British Columbia, Canada, the Ministry of Education stipulates that the IEP must set out:

1. present level of educational performance (including strengths and needs);

2. goals that correspond to the curricular areas that are adapted or modified;

3. goals for students that reflect their identified Ministry category;

4. measurable objectives that focus on performance and observable behaviour;

5. teaching strategies, materials and support required to reach the stated objectives;

6. names of the people responsible for implementing the plan;

7. where the plan will be implemented;

8. the means of assessment and evaluation; and

9. the period of time and a process for reviewing the IEP.

Long-term goals are expressed in the IEP as broad, general statements of learning outcomes that address the prioritized needs of the student. Goals are designed to be challenging but achievable—based on the student's needs—and are positive statements about what the student will learn rather than what will be taught.

The IEP: a developmental perspective

From a developmental perspective, the IEP definitely falls short! What is missing from it is any real recognition of the importance of maturational processes—in particular, the vital role that connectedness plays in the child's education. Although 'social' and 'emotional' are categories considered in goal-setting, no real attention is given, either in the process or the IEP document itself, to the importance of emotion as the engine of maturation. Instead, the emphasis of the IEP is on skills, what the child will learn, and the teaching strategies and methods used. Steve Cairns, a recently retired school principal, describes it thus:

"Currently, connectedness is a by-product of an IEP. The IEP, in its very essence, brings focus to the child's needs. But it is due to the child's negative behaviour and/or poor social or academic development that he will receive attention through a network of care. What a backward way of achieving care from adults—the very care that should have been there in the beginning for 'normal' development! In our IEPs at Morley Elementary, we worked on the principle of 'reach then teach'. Our belief is that emotional needs must first be met in order to ensure sustained social and academic development."

Essentially, today's IEPs address student disabilities or deficits rather than student assets. All too often, goals and objectives set in IEPs indicate that we are reacting to symptoms rather than responding proactively to the child. They indicate a lack of patience, awareness and understanding that relationship is at the heart of our current parenting and teaching difficulties and, also, at the heart of the solution. They indicate that we are reading a child only through numbers and assessments rather than organically through the lens of connectedness.

Key questions

1. What do children require in order to realize their potential?
Firstly, they are meant to be connected with adults, to depend on us and be taken care of by us. They need to emerge as separate beings, full of their own ideas, intentions, meanings, aspirations and values. They need to adapt to lack and loss in order to develop the resilience to handle reality.

2. What should an IEP measure? In addition to measuring social and academic growth, the IEP should measure adaptive, emergent and integrative development. For example, is there evidence of the child feeling sadness at the things in life he/she cannot control/change? Is the child able to move from mad to sad? Is there evidence that he/she can say "I'm scared"? Is there evidence of contact and closeness with adults?

3. What do we want the child to be able to do? The child is expected to demonstrate adaptive, integrative and emergent qualities. Clearly, if there is little evidence of these qualities emerging, then it is necessary for adults to focus on the relationship, spend more time with the child, and be physically closer to him or her. It is imperative that they focus on sameness and identity (what they share in common), belonging and loyalty, approval and significance, warmth and love, and finally being seen (known).

4. What can adults do to help the child be successful? IEPs must be asset-based. Ideally, each student should have a personal education plan (PEP) that speaks richly to the child's strengths and preferences and that reflects his/her 'sparks'. PEPs should reflect the fact that adults are the child's anchor and advocate. The goals and strategies need to include the expectation that teachers, staff and parents exhibit happiness to see the child and enjoy being with him/her. It is crucial that the IEPs indicate that we are practising simple greeting rituals such as collecting, bridging and matchmaking.[18]

---

18   Neufeld and Mate, 2005

'Collecting' means engaging the child's attachment instincts by greeting and engaging the child in a friendly way, making eye contact, gaining their attention and interest, keeping them close and letting them know they matter to us.

'Bridging' involves protecting and preserving relationships. When a child faces separation, bridging preserves the connection by drawing attention to what stays the same and when you will see the child again. For example, I might say: "I look forward to seeing you on Monday." I might even give the child something personal of mine to hang onto as a reminder of me, such as a trinket or a book to read.

'Matchmaking' means creating a village for a child. Matchmaking a child with someone responsible for him/her facilitates the relationship through introduction. A teacher in the matchmaking role might facilitate relationships for the child with other teachers and staff members, and make it easy for them to like each other, perhaps through compliments—for example: "Your teacher has said great things about you." It is important for the child to see the matchmaker in a friendly interaction with the person to whom the child is being matched.

John's story illustrates matchmaking, collecting and bridging.

John's story
by Troy Closs

John is a 9-year-old boy with ASD. He was frequently running and screaming in the halls, refusing to go to class, leaving the school premises and exhibiting myriad other behaviours that would inevitably land him at the office. This is ultimately where he spent most of his time. He was segregated from his classmates and had no connection to the classroom teacher or the educational assistant. John did, however, have one very important teacher in the school with whom he had connected. Unfortunately, John was in another teacher's class and had been taking his cues from his peers in the alternative education program.

I started working with John three months into the school year. Realizing that the only way for me to cultivate a relationship with him was by matching him with his previous teacher, I quickly set up a plan that would see John connecting with her every morning and going through the same morning rituals as in the previous year. John would enter the room and the teacher would say: "Good morning" and then the entire class would turn toward him and, in unison, would say: "Good morning, John." We would laugh together and share stories with the class. This affirmed for John that we were cool and that our channels of communication were open. John knew that he was now accountable to both of us. This gave John both a morning ritual and an opportunity to start his day with success.

When I was first introduced to John, he was having a very difficult time becoming integrated into his classroom. He would consistently refuse to go to class and would act out while in class by being loud and disruptive. My goal was to integrate him into the classroom, help him to develop appropriate relationships with his peers and have him serve as a role model for others. I already had a strong basis for attachment with John because of the fact that I have two boys of my own who are the same age as him. Sharing stories about my boys that he could relate to was invaluable in terms of forging our attachment.

When confronted with any demands or ultimatums, or when asked to make restitution, John would resist. He would make the tightest face possible and stare directly into space as if you were no longer there. I once told John that if he did not stop referring to his pencil as a "weapon", I would take the pencil from him. John, after a short pause, slowly looked up at me and with the most defiant voice possible said, "weapon". I knew what I had done. I had put John directly into a defensive position by giving him an ultimatum without first establishing an attachment. I had set myself up for no other possible response. I knew from then on that a warm heart and a consistent relational approach would be the best vehicle for me.

After several weeks of this approach, with the willingness of other staff to jump on board, John was in class full days and, even though he was allowed to request breaks, he always chose to stay in class. One of the turning points for John happened when it was time for a class meeting on the carpet and John joined in, as usual. Until this day, John had always been allowed to 'pass' when it came to his turn to speak. On this day, the teacher decided to challenge John a little and prompted him to give a temperature reading of how he was feeling (1 = not great, 10 = great). All John had to do was give a number and he could pass to someone else. The more the teacher prompted John, the more John went into a defensive position. His head went down, his face turned red and you could see that he was uncomfortable. After about a minute, the teacher stopped prompting John and the meeting went on. Sensing that John was distressed, I took him outside the classroom and sat with him in the office with my arm around him. I asked him why he was so stressed about speaking on the carpet. John looked up at me with watery eyes and said, "I am shy." He began to cry.

John's confiding in me and finding his tears was an important juncture in our relationship. He had shared his vulnerability with me. This confirmed to me that our relationship had evolved. I had already established other connections for him throughout the school, so continuing to play matchmaker was natural and easy.

Although John's progress has been remarkable, he still struggles when I am not there. I have been addressing this with John by assuring him that, although I may be physically absent, that does not mean that I don't care about him or that my thoughts are not with him. I attempt to bridge the time we will be apart by focusing on when I will be back and how/when I will be thinking about him while I am gone.

Overall, John has come a long way and is continuing to flourish. He now spends his whole day with his class, shares on the carpet, has a little buddy that he reads to, participates in gym (without threatening to pull the fire alarm), seeks out and initiates new friendships, and is our custodian's assistant. Most importantly, he has a village around him who he believes care about him.

IEPs that highlight positive things about the child and his good intentions set the stage for the parent to see the child in a different way. Well-thought-out education plans address and celebrate places of touch-down grounding for the child—their safe places. They indicate that children need time and space, how vital it is that we teach children strategies to help them deal with frustration, and that frustration is a perfectly natural emotion. Adults need to model what it is to be confused and vulnerable and that it is okay to feel/express one's vulnerabilities.

The language of the education plan should highlight our role as a coach. If we truly believe that we are a child's best opportunity for achieving maturation, we need to show up and be available when needed.

It is imperative that educators be mindful that imposing consequences can blind us to safe, natural and effective ways of changing behaviour. Often, they create adversarial relationships and emotional hardening of our children. I encourage you to embrace rituals and rules that safeguard healthy connection and make it easy for children to attach fully and deeply to us. Rather than preoccupying ourselves with techniques and prescriptive programs, we need to focus on being stewards of children's hearts and fulfil their need to be connected. This will help to immunize them against life's misfortunes and remove impediments to maturation.

Steve Cairns best describes our role as responsible educators:

"If we didn't invest in children's emotional development so they could first come to a place of rest, we would never get anywhere with their social and academic development. At Morley, we knew this was a long, slow process that was dependent upon teachers and other adults looking at IEPs—and all other plans—with a critical eye for what they needed to do first so that the child could do what he/she needed to do—namely mature. It had to happen in that order. We even went further to say that if a child was not achieving socially or academically, that was cause for us to review and revamp the plan. Our efforts were more focused on monitoring and supporting staff, parents and other significant adults than on the child. The adults were the ones that needed to be doing the 'right' things so the child could trust in our lead. Those in the lead did indeed have the child's best interests at heart. No actions were punitive or had pointless consequences. These children had already experienced too much of that type of lead in their lives. It took careful, consistent, networked, responsible adult leadership to bring them to a place of rest and trust. This meant constantly reinforcing the actions of the adults so they did not become distracted by the secondary goals of academic achievement. Nor could we let weak social skills interfere with our primary goal: we were on a mission to constantly, patiently, and lovingly return the goslings to the row behind the goose or the gander.

"Our report cards were masterpieces of this intent. All conferences and staff meetings focused on the actions of the adults and parents to build on the emotional achievements, while skilfully recognizing social and academic achievements. IEPs were only as good as the work we did in connectedness."

10. Understanding the emotional roots of behaviour

I do not need anger management.
I simply need to be understood.
—**Bev Ogilvie**

Folks in my school district often ask me who needs a Functional Behavioural Assessment (FBA). My answer? All students who fall under the British Columbia Ministry of Education designation of moderate or severe behavioural problems, or any student who is exhibiting challenging behaviour, require an FBA.

According to the BC Ministry of Education, the primary purpose of an FBA is to:

1. bring insight and clarity into the reasons for the challenging behaviour;

2. understand the structure and function of challenging behaviour in order to teach and promote healthier behaviour;

3. promote effective staff responses so challenging behaviour can be eliminated or modified to facilitate the teaching of healthier behaviours;

4. individualize and structure students' learning environments in order to fully support them in their educational needs; and

5. maximize the effectiveness and efficiency of behavioural support.

Based on the assumptions that behaviour is a form of communication and that all behaviour serves some purpose, the FBA process is meant to identify the perceived function that a specific behaviour serves—for example, to get something or to escape from/avoid something. School

86

personnel gather information to help them identify patterns that trigger and maintain the behaviour. Members of staff identify what factors—such as antecedents and consequences—might be associated with the behaviour. Antecedents are stimuli that trigger or predict the behaviour. Consequences are what happen immediately afterwards, as a result of the behaviour. The behaviour is described in terms of what it looks like, how often it happens, how long it lasts, and how severe or dangerous it is. The Behaviour Intervention Plan is a specifically written and purposefully organized plan designed to:

1. identify preventive practices and replacement behaviours that teachers and supporting personnel can implement to increase appropriate behaviour and decrease inappropriate behaviour;

2. provide proactive strategies that allow individual students to access appropriate educational environments in order to meet their needs;

3. identify positive and negative consequences along with practices for maintaining positive appropriate behaviour; and

4. value the uniqueness of each child, as well as their strengths and weaknesses.

FBAs address problematic behaviour and issues around learning and lack of skills. Much attention is placed on shaping or teaching replacement behaviours for non-compliance, aggression, learning problems, impulsive behaviour and disruptive or interfering behaviour. Many of the strategies and goals outlined in the FBA are about roles, practices and programs.

What is missing in the FBA is attention to emotion and the all-important goal of realizing human potential. (See Appendix 4 for strategies relating to connectedness for FBAs, as well as for IEPs.) As discussed in Chapter 4, the realization of human potential is a process of maturation, which results in the ability to simultaneously handle togetherness and separation and to function independently. There are three elements in the maturation process: adaptive, integrative and emergent.

1. Adaptive: the ability to overcome adversity, which evolves as a result of encounters with futility—that is, from coming to terms with something that cannot be changed.

2. Integrative: the ability to practise self-control and consideration in a social setting.

3. Emergent: the ability to exist as a separate, viable being.

Key question

From a developmental perspective, where might emphasis be placed in order to understand where the child is, in terms of his maturation?

My colleague, Lis Kroeker, and I adapted Neufeld's work on maturation to create the following developmental inventory, which gives consideration to arrested maturation or developmental stuckness in the areas of adaptive, integrative and emergent functioning.

Functional developmental inventory (Ogilvie & Kroeker, 2009)

Student name: School/program:

Grade/age: Date of assessment: Teacher:

Emergence (i.e., a child standing on his/her own two feet)

Emergence is the life process of differentiation whereby a child achieves viability as a separate being. It is characterized by a 'venturing forth' kind of energy that arises spontaneously from within the developing child. The process of emergence is not inevitable. It depends on a child's relational needs being met and it gives rise to many of the attributes we find desirable in a child: a sense of responsibility, accountability, curiosity, interest, boundaries, respect for others, individuality and personhood.

Use the following key to rate the child's emergent process:

5= always; 4 = most of the time; 3= regularly; 2= sometimes; 1=rarely

Level of child's emergence	5	4	3	2	1
Is curious; learns new material					
Looks at/opens up to unfamiliar topics or activities					
Is inclined to figure things out by him/herself					
Has the aspiration to realize own potential as a learner					
Tends to come up with own ideas					
Takes initiative and responsibility					
Has adequate boundaries					
Has a sense of separateness from peers					
Is not easily bored					

Integrative functioning (i.e., social integration; taking into account the perspective of another)

Integrative functioning involves the mixing of different elements of the personality to create a new whole—for example, hostile emotions can be integrated with compassion or anxiety. This mixing produces perspective, balance and emotional and social maturity. The essence of integration, in the social realm, is mixing without blending, or togetherness without the loss of separateness. This requires sufficient prior differentiation by the child so that he/she can experience togetherness without losing his/her sense of self.

Level of child's integrative functioning	5	4	3	2	1
Not a black-and-white thinker. Has mixed feelings					
Has extreme reactions					
Considers context or more than one consideration at a time when solving problems					
Delays gratification/makes sacrifices towards a goal					
Has ability to operate out of two reference points at one time (on the one hand, on the other hand...)					
Seems capable of courage or patience					
Understands other points of view					
Is fair, considerate, empathic					
Mixes well with others					

Adaptation (i.e., resilience)

The adaptive process refers to how a child develops emotionally or learns new realities as a result of coming to terms with something that cannot be changed. This is the process by which children learn from their mistakes, benefit from failure, and are changed for the better by adversity.

Level of child's adaptation	5	4	3	2	1
Learns from trial and error					
Transcends any handicaps or existing disabilities					
Benefits from having mistakes or failures pointed out					
Learns from consequences					
Moves on/rises above when things do not work					
Cries, feels the sadness of what does not work					
Is resourceful/resolves conflict and avoids trouble					
Handles adversity					
Accepts limits or restrictions					
Is not easily provoked					
Is not led astray					

In contrast to the FBA (which focuses on problematic behaviour or a diagnosed disorder), a Functional Developmental Inventory (FDI) addresses the pivotal factor of emotion. While the FBA is all about cognition, replacement behaviours and consequences, the FDI examines the emotional impediments to maturation. With the FDI, the context is one of relationship, not behaviour. Growth and development happen as a result of being in deeply fulfilling relationships with adults.

The following story illustrates how connecting with children brings us face to face with our own emotions, impulsiveness and inner conflict. It will be necessary for us to feel our sadness and disappointment when things do not go our way. Otherwise, we risk becoming emotionally hardened ourselves, becoming rigid and ineffective. We will need to find compassion for ourselves, to accept that we are fallible and that, at times, our frustration will get the better of us. As this story illustrates, amid our own mixed feelings, we can achieve clarity, balance and perspective.

Softening our hearts as teachers
by Lis Kroeker

The students sat at the front of the classroom, facing the teachers. Four students sharing their stories; 30 teachers watching, listening. We had asked the students from the Alternative Education Program to come and share their stories with these teachers. They came full of mixed feelings, determined to give voice to their stories so that others could be spared from the pain and the loneliness that they had experienced throughout their school years.

As the students spoke, themes started to emerge in their stories— not feeling as if they belonged; not perceiving that there were adults in the school that cared; being punished without ever having had the chance to share their side; frustration gone foul; despair; being misunderstood; and lost childhoods as they navigated poverty, abuse, and substance abuse issues generated by those who were supposed to be taking care of them.

We had gone over the questions with the students prior to the panel presentation, had given them the choice of not answering if they didn't feel safe responding, and told them that they could leave at any point. It was all meant to make them feel safe. What we didn't anticipate as we planned for this safety was how the teachers would respond. With tears in my eyes, I looked around the room and noticed some of the teachers crying, while others became agitated. The more vulnerable the stories, the more their agitation grew. And then the attack began. They started to point at the student and ask them questions. They started to accuse them. Amazingly, the students held on to themselves, and spoke clearly and eloquently about their plight. Their own current teachers were sitting at the table closest to them, and I could see the students taking their cues from them.

As I drove home that evening, I was angry. How could grown-up, intelligent adults attack tender and young souls like this? Where were their instincts to protect? Finally, I found myself full of sadness for the children and their stories. I felt sadness for the teachers who were so defended against vulnerability that they could not go to a place of generosity. How do we soften the hearts of teachers? How do we make it safe for them to feel the sadness of what they cannot or could not change? How do we invite them to a place of rest so that they can hear their hearts again? As I chatted with colleagues, I realized that the teachers were unable to hear the stories because of their own vulnerabilities. I realized that if I wanted to be effective in helping the teachers to come alongside the students, I would have to somehow find a way to make it safe for them to feel their sadness.

I recently presented a workshop to teachers in another district—this time, without any students. Determined to learn from my previous experience, I walked the teachers through a process of exploration. We talked about the behaviours that they observed and found the most difficult, and what that was like for them. We talked about what they interpreted the behaviour to mean, and what that felt like to them. As we listed the behaviours, you could feel the energy in the room. As we listed the interpretations, you could feel it even more. "It tells me that she doesn't care." "It tells me that she doesn't value what I do for her." "It tells me that this is too much for me." And then feelings started to emerge. "I feel angry." "I feel disappointed." "I feel inadequate." "I feel frustrated." "I feel disengaged." "I feel hurt." "I feel sad."

I held them in those feelings for a bit, and the energy changed. Suddenly, there was silence in the room. There was a sadness that took over the whole group. And then I said to them: "How would your thinking change if I told you that this child is developmentally stuck, that while he is 16 years old, he is really only functioning like a four-year-old?" And one of the teachers—one of the ones that had been the loudest in terms of her feelings of frustration—whispered to me: "It would move to compassion."

I went back to the first group of teachers—the ones who had heard the students—and I did the same thing. I invited them to be aware of their feelings and I held them there, and something moved. Something shifted. Their hearts had softened as well.

What follows is another story about keeping our hearts soft, as adults:

The boy who didn't exist
by Lis Kroeker

I drove down the little lane towards the house in the country and I could see a little boy waiting for me. The farm was vast. The house was large and dark. The boy was little, somehow not really matching his surroundings.

Peter had been suspended from the school on the day before the Christmas holidays. His alarm and frustration had escalated to the point that it was impossible to get him to do anything. Any request coming from an adult was met with the exact opposite behaviour; any request for a conversation was followed by nasty words, accusations and threats. Peter had been identified as a bully in our school. He walked around looking for more vulnerable students, targeting them with physical and verbal abuse. He was defiant towards teachers and adults, including his mom, and demanded that his requests and wants be met. He made threats when things were not going his way.

I asked the principal if I could have a private meeting with him. There had already been frequent meetings with Peter but he had always shut down and the adults had left, filled with frustration. His parents had tried to take him to another school, but no school that knew of his reputation was prepared to take him. After some discussion, the principal agreed to call the parents to see if they would allow him to see me. They agreed, but said that they would not bring him to the school; if I wanted to talk to him, I would have to pick him up and bring him home afterwards.

As I drove towards his home, I spotted Peter waiting for me. Watching me carefully, he climbed into my car with a hesitant "hello". We drove and chatted while we munched on grapes that I had bought on the way. We talked about the holidays, about the chickens on his property and who got to feed them, about his new dog Wolf (and how much bigger he was than my little Pomeranian), and about his dirt bike. I was doing everything I could to collect him and to help him connect with me.

Once we got to my office, I asked him to make a picture of what he thought was happening. I was looking for integrative functioning. Could he see both sides of the issue? Could he talk from the 'other side' of the problem? I wanted to see if he could feel his sadness about what wasn't working. I drew a little heart on the paper and asked him what his story felt like. He coloured the whole heart in black. "It feels like I am being swallowed into a big black hole into nothingness," he said. Then he whispered quietly, "I feel like I don't exist."

Peter's counterwill (which is the human instinct to resist pressure and coercion, and serves by keeping children from being unduly influenced by those they are not attached to) started to make sense to me. His brain was protecting him against a sense of vulnerability that was too overwhelming. He was defensive about being attached to any of the adults in his life. Defending against vulnerability is a protective mechanism involving emotional and perceptual filters that screen out information that the person would find too wounding or painful. There was something in this little boy's life that was making it too hard to feel.

I realized that what I needed to do was to somehow soften the hearts of the adults towards this little boy. It was crucial for us to stop seeing him as the bad boy who would not do our bidding and, instead, to see the little boy that needed us to invite him to exist in our caring presence. We needed to see how incredibly vulnerable and defensive he was. We needed to yearn for him, and seek to be in a right relationship with him so he could depend on us.

Last night, my teaching partner was shopping for groceries after work. As she was selecting apples, she heard a little voice calling her name. When she looked up, she saw Peter running towards her with the greatest smile on his face. "I am coming back to the school tomorrow!" he announced to her. "I can't wait to be back with all of you again!"

My yearning is that we'll be able to keep our hearts soft towards this little boy as we seek to create a school community that is safe and welcoming to all kids.

11. The essence of meeting needs: a school principal's perspective

Written by Steve Cairns

Make the system meet the needs of the child; do not make the child meet the needs of the system.
—**Steve Cairns**

In 2003, Bev Ogilvie and I created an initiative called Project Hope. Bev was the District Counsellor and I was the new administrator of an inner-city school. The fundamental premise of this project was that every child should possess feelings of belonging, resilience and hope. Feelings of belonging come from being safe, cared for and nurtured by the significant adults in one's life. Resilience is the ability to survive and thrive in one's environment. Hope is a feeling that is generated from the belief that one may live a happy, healthy life.

At that time, we believed that our students were some of the most vulnerable in the district. Poverty, community decay and, often, their personal family experience as refugees led us to believe that these children were highly at-risk. We believed that the majority of these children needed to feel that they belonged—that they were safe in our school and in their community. We wanted to help them meet their basic needs and we intended to connect them with significant adults in the school and in the community who could nurture and care for them.

We took our vision to the school staff and to the systems and organizations in the community. School staff were hesitant to take on another role in the lives of these children. Community members regarded us with confusion and even mistrust. They seemed to feel that they were already doing all that could be done, and that the education system had already taken on many of the roles that they believed were rightly the responsibility of parents and family. The community believed that, with the systems they had, they had a pretty good handle on helping children and families meet their basic needs of food, clothing and shelter.

In fact, what they said was true. Everyone was doing the best they could within the mandate of their respective system. Nevertheless, despite the teachers' best intentions, we felt that children were not getting what they deeply needed. Today, we refer to this way of operating as a 'system of silos'. Each organization was doing 'its thing' but not within the culture of Project Hope—namely, providing children with feelings of belonging, resilience and hope.

We now know that the children of Project Hope were actually the exposed edge of a social wound that ran much deeper than we ever wanted to believe. At-risk children populate every community, regardless of its socio-economic status, its urban or rural nature, or its ethnic or cultural predominance. Too many children today do not feel that they belong; they do not possess the qualities necessary to feel resilient, and they feel a diminishing sense of hope for their future.

The good news is that we learned from Project Hope. We have found a way into the silos of school and community and how to connect them. The language of this culture states the following:

1. All children are our children.

2. Family is the most important organization of all.

3. Adults must always be in the lead.

4. Adults guide, mentor, and become the moral compass for, the child.

5. Adults must share the responsibility of raising the child within a cultural agreement.

6. A cultural agreement begins with a shared language that defines the values, beliefs and practices that nurture the healthy development of the child.

7. It is as important that the adults in a child's life be connected

with each other as it is that the child be connected with each adult.

8. Community is defined by the adults who work as a team to raise the child.

9. Community begins with the family and expands as adults guide children into the world.

10. School is the centre of community.

11. Systems must meet the needs of the child, rather than the child meeting the needs of the systems.

12. When we have a child's heart, we can engage his/her mind.

13. Right relationships are safe, secure and nurturing for the child.

14. Right relationships will move us all closer to a healthier future.

As Project Hope matured, the school and community began to work with a shared language. Practices addressed the emotional needs first, which enabled us to meet the unique social and intellectual needs of each child. Over time, we began to witness the purposeful and intentional networking of each child's significant adults so that they could best meet the needs of the child.

The adult network focused on nurturing the development of the whole child. To best facilitate the networking process, we created a vehicle that we called an NCP (Network Connection Plan) (see Appendix 5). The NCP identified the significant adults in a child's life. The first goal of the NCP was to have each adult invite the child into a relationship. Keeping the adults connected, informed and working together was a critical part of this process.

The success of our work became clear in the elementary school setting and its community, as staff and community began to embrace the new culture. Children and families described their feelings of belonging in the school and the community. They felt safe and welcome. They felt significant. Life remained challenging for many children and families but their growing sense of resilience brought them to a more optimistic feeling about their future.

Further evidence of the success occurred when the secondary school to which many of our elementary students transitioned was recognized with the prestigious ASCD 2012 Award for the Development of the Whole Child. Although we cannot take the credit for the great work that brought them this honour, we did, in fact, meet with a cohort of the secondary school staff every week to explore the new culture. We also believed that the children were now being nurtured by the community in the transition to the secondary setting. The supportive forces from the larger community, a visionary school administrator and a dedicated school staff combined to make this complex school a system that always endeavoured to meet the needs of the child by adjusting the needs of the system.

Another example of the power of the culture of connectedness began in the summer of 2012, when we began to work with a large elementary school outside of our district in an upscale community. With our support, the admin team and staff aligned the culture of the school to meet the emotional needs of the children. One year later, in the summer of 2013, the administrator of that school proudly presented her emotionally charged story describing the transformative powers of the culture in her school. The capacity audience was transfixed by her keynote address, detailing the journey of one student's transformation from exclusion to inclusion as the community learned to embrace his unique needs.

These are the successes with which we are most intimately aware. Similar stories are emerging throughout BC and other provinces. The following is an outline of how the culture can develop within any school community.

Why

In identifying the underpinnings of the vision that we wish to cultivate, the focus is on what we want for our children, youth and families and why it is so important to our collective future. The 14 points mentioned above are a good place to begin the affirmative view of our work. We refer to the 'hard' work that comes with changing a paradigm as 'heart' work.

How

When you begin to create a shared vision with staff, parents and community, it is important to emphasize the fact that you are not offering a new program but simply a new way to contextualize how we should do our adult work. How to cast that vision is truly the art of leadership. To effectively cast the vision, a leader must know the research and knowledge that support a vision but, more importantly, the leader must first believe in the vision and then inspire others to fulfill it.

The 'how' phase has only one goal, which is to establish the language that will define the building blocks of the cultural agreement—namely, the beliefs, values and practices of the culture. Achieving that singular goal will facilitate the process of 'how'. The aim is to be strategic, purposeful and intentional, to create the conditions and the inspiration required to develop and sustain the culture.

The first condition of 'how' is to provide regular collaborative time. Collaboration time for the staff of community organizations (schools, services, community organizations…) is essential to share the language and to explore the beliefs, values and practices that tell the stories of what is working and what is not working. In creating the culture, storytelling is the 'meaning-making' process. Stories can clarify, authenticate and inspire. Furthermore, staff must feel safe to try something, and then share their findings, successes and frustrations. Together, the staff can create 'meaning' as they share the responsibility of applying the culture of the village. Perhaps most importantly, the staff must find the creativity and courage to explore what it means to make the system meet the needs of the child rather than making the child meet the needs of the system.

Every group will have to determine how they will allocate regular collaboration time. In the school setting, changing bell schedules can free up an hour each week. Collaboration time must occur weekly or bi-weekly. If the time between sessions stretches past once every two weeks, then the energy and drive are in danger of being lost to the tyranny of the emergent.

At the same time, administrators are encouraged to take advantage of every assembly, newsletter, bulletin… whatever, whenever… to plant the words of the new language in the vocabularies of all who will engage the children in the culture.

What

Typically, 'what' refers to evidence or outcomes, which are very important, especially when taking the vision forward to policy-makers and leaders. In our experience, 'what' is more than the evidence. It is the piece that achieves systemic sustainability through inspiration. When others are inspired, they feel a sense of ownership and personal commitment. Inspiration keeps the commitment and belief in the culture strong and robust.

One of the defining qualities of humans is our ability to envision a better future and strategically, purposefully and intentionally work to achieve it. We know that parents all over the world want their children to be happy, safe and healthy. Our individual time and ability to affect the future is small, but our collective time, employed in a healthy and enduring way, is immense.

Part 2. Finding the connector in you

12. Be crazy about children

Every child requires someone in his or her life
who is absolutely crazy about them.
—Urie Bronfenbrenner

If we want children to make a mark on the world, we need to let them know that they make their mark in *our* world. We need to let them know that they matter to us and bring us joy. We rejoice in their existence. We cherish them. In a nutshell, they light up our world.

It is imperative that we, as educators, find that place in ourselves where we believe children are worth it. It is easier to find that place within us if we believe we are worth it ourselves. Children can lean on us. We can take it. Their problems are our problems and together we'll prevail. We'll find a way.

Fran's message in her upcoming story is plain and simple. She endeavours to let each child in the school know that she is crazy about them just because of who they are. No explanation is necessary. By inviting them to exist in her presence—to simply be with her—she allows them to feel true acceptance. They are each significant to her in their own way. They're 'keepers'... just because.

ConnectZones

by Fran De Tracie

I am an elementary school custodian. My favourite times are when kids are changing classrooms. Actually, it can be any time students are in the hall for any reason at all: washroom trips, drinks at the fountain or returning books to the library—anything that serves as an excuse for me to connect. And it doesn't matter what the issue is; it is an important opportunity for me to really connect with the 'fringe kids'. The kids who have balanced, stable lives enjoy it too, because they feel good when someone takes an interest in, for instance, their basketball scoring average or dance routines. It can be as simple as a friendly greeting.

Fringe kids are my specialty. They become fringe kids because they believe that they don't matter enough to warrant any quality attention. This belief pervades their expectations of others. You can spot them easily. They are the ones who are too shy to make eye contact, to speak up or even speak at all. They rarely initiate anything with adults but often stir up trouble in the playground, then sit back and watch the drama. They are the ones writing on bathroom walls, carving up their desks, puncturing balls. They are the ones who become the bullies of tomorrow. Many bullies are passive-aggressive types who do not stand out like the stereotypical bully. They are the ones who stand by and laugh while kids are being victimized.

With a little love and interest in them when they are young, we can make a difference. We've all become so phobic of touch that we are afraid of the most natural tendencies—even to give a kid a hug. That kid will let you know whether he/she is comfortable or not. A few moments is all most kids need. Let's take the time to give them that extra moment. Pushing hair out of their eyes, straightening a collar, catching an untied shoelace could make the difference between a bully and a hero, down the line.

Key points

1. It is important that adults offer children unconditional love and acceptance.

2. It is vital that schools become ConnectZones—places where children, youth and adults are attended to, valued and accepted.

3. ConnectZones need to:

   - be welcoming, nurturing arenas of infinite possibilities that foster a sense of rootedness, harmony, belonging and connection;

   - value meaningful relationships, physical and emotional safety, security, exploration, self-expression, growth and maturation;

   - represent communities of care;

   - embrace trusting and caring relationships.

   - re-establish resiliency by reconnecting to our grounding, our resources and one another;[19]

   - promote the maintenance of personal boundaries and an awareness of when to attend to our own self-care; and

   - promote the protective practice of heartfelt, empathic engagement.

---

19   Russell, 2013

13. Walking the talk of connectedness as a true leader

Have the courage to be vulnerable... it transforms the way we live, love, parent and lead.
—Brené Brown

Taking a serious look at these questions for educators will help you to focus on what you need to do to become a connected leader, if you so desire.

1. What is your IEP?

2. What are you expected to be able to do, to walk the talk of connectedness in schools?

3. What has to happen for you to get there?

4. What do you need to do to become emergent, to feel a sense of agency and responsibility to practise connectedness, and to aspire to realize your potential as a connector?

Leadership requires having the courage to be vulnerable and the conviction to transform the system. It requires an understanding that, although schools get a lot of things right, they also nurse policies and practices that do not put relationships first and that undermine the development of empathy. It requires us to be self-critical about our role in perpetuating practices and processes that cause harm to others or oppress families and each other.

Leadership means committing to the building of community as a process, not an entity, with the understanding that it is created through collaboration and respect. It requires us to acknowledge that relationships, not programs, are the agents of change and that we need to get out of our silos and work together. It requires our commitment to the development of more empathy in ourselves and others.

As realizers of change, we must create the space for change. We must look hard at the unwritten curriculum in our schools and deliver the proper goods, which go beyond the lesson plan. To walk the talk of connectedness in schools is to view complex and deeply personal relationships as the foundation of effective teaching. It means viewing children as creatures of attachment and relational learners. It means acknowledging that a child's brain needs more than words, lessons and curricular activities. It needs love and friendship, freedom to play, and rest.

To walk the talk of connectedness in schools is to champion caring relationships. It is about guiding and inspiring children and allowing them to feel your warmth. You will attend to goodbye and greeting rituals, introductions, matchmaking and bridging that which could divide (see Chapter 9). You will embrace the roots of attachment (see Rebecca's story in Chapter 2) through:

1. being with
2. sameness—what you share in common with your students
3. belonging and loyalty
4. feelings of significance
5. love
6. being known

In the context of application, as an educator, you might use/refer to a particular developmental attachment theory, but you are always teaching about the child to the parent, colleague or community member who may need to see the child in a different way and align with his or her best qualities. You will connect:

1. research to practice
2. children to caregivers
3. schools to community

To find the connector in you, your goal is to be curious, gentle and engaged. You will need to make room for the part of you that feels trapped and frustrated. Often, you may feel like a ping pong ball, alternating between having warm feelings for children when they behave, and disliking them when they don't. You may feel like a pushover, one moment and, the next, your heart might be frozen.

You may feel out of control and want to revert to relying upon old, familiar ways of doing things, or whatever program is popular at the time. Maybe you have become expert at finding experts or have been programmed to find programs. Perhaps you have doubted your own intuition for so long that you automatically look outside of yourself for comfort and the skills you feel you may be lacking.

You may be desperate and want to give up. You may have arrived at the belief that you teach the way you do because it's not possible to teach any other way. But it is in these moments of desperation and confusion that a different way of teaching—and of living—may be revealed to you. It is typically at these times that you are open to questioning what you've never questioned.

These are the times, when you realize things are not working, that you may decide you want something different and to operate differently. To walk the talk of connectedness, you will need to get back in touch with who you really are—your true nature, your essence and your needs as a social being. By looking within, you will not go without. You will come to trust your intuition, your longings, your dreams and your choices. You will feel in control and, when left to your own devices and intuition, you can trust yourself!

The COLT model

I developed the COLT model in 2012. It summarizes who we are, our focus, and what we do when we are at our best as connectors. It speaks to 'right relationships' and soft hearts. It promotes nurturing networks, innovation and development from the inside out. It speaks to finding the voices of children and families, and to bridging schools and communities and homes. As a model, it addresses the 'how' and the 'why'—that is, building relationships, communities of care, inspirational leaders and systemic change.

COLT stands for:

C – compassion, calm, connection, courage, confidence, collaborative process, champions, catalyst, community, conversations, communication, creativity, collecting

O – open, organization (the most important one being family), opportunities, owners (of our future)

L – love, language (of quality), leadership, link

T – thriving, togetherness, trust, tools (of the mind), teaching, tolerance

To summarize, walking the talk of connectedness as a true leader means nurturing a health-promoting school environment in which you strive to:

- facilitate meaningful connections between students, staff, parents and community members;

- ensure that students feel safe from physical and emotional harm, secure in their relationships with teachers and peers, and valued as important members of their school;

- engage a broad range of people and different voices to contribute to the change; and

- flatten the hierarchy by taking an appreciative approach to change that is creative and generative, and by asking how community members can engage in creating compassionate children and caring communities.

The following story illustrates community at its best.

The secret life of mothers and teachers

by Lis Kroeker

"I think he's 'gone to the bathroom'," said my teaching partner as she held on to baby Jake. There was some laughter in the room, as well as stories of how this always happens at the most inopportune time (we all had stories of putting babies into their car seats only to hear and smell the next job to be done!). Grandma laughed and offered to change the diaper. The baby's mom looked relieved and Aiden, baby Jake's cousin, showed us his latest Lego creation, oblivious to what was going on.

I felt like a visitor in somebody's living room, with babies held, children playing and mothers, aunties and grandmas visiting. Except that it wasn't a living room. It was my counselling office in our little country school. And we were not there just visiting and telling stories. We were there to go over the Psycho-Educational Assessment that had been done on Aiden in an attempt to come to a better understanding of how he was processing information.

The school psychologist had refused to come to the meeting to report, because she didn't want so many people there. She only wanted to meet with Aiden's mom. Aiden's mom, who is vulnerable herself, had asked (after much nurturing from us, in the recent past) that we be there with her during the process. She had invited grandma, her sister and baby Jake, as well as the classroom teacher and the special education teacher. She had also invited me, the area counsellor. She wanted all of us there because, in her heart, she sensed that we were her son's advocates. Without the school psychologist being present, I was left to do the reporting.

Between burps, diaper changes, Lego figures and stories from the sandbox, I slowly went over the report. I drew, I sketched and I explained. How do you break the news that a child's ability profile is severely compromised? How do you inject hope into the story of a child who scores desperately low in areas so vital to survival in our society?

We talked, we wondered and we thought of ideas. We held on to the belief that, in the safe, caring context, we could compensate for what Aiden couldn't do, just now, so that he could come to a place of rest. We talked about what was missing for him, in terms of integrative and adaptive functioning, and we talked about what we could offer him as his adults. We laughed and we cried.

The meeting took longer than other reporting meetings I have attended. We left full of hope, talking about how we believed that we could see emergence in this child, and we encouraged each other to observe Aiden from the inside out. It was not a clinical meeting where numbers and verdicts of the future were presented. It was a meeting where we not only supported Aiden, but Aiden's mom, as well. It was a beautiful picture of a community coming together to support the development of one of its children.

Key points

1. Lis modelled the fact that the relationship with the child and the family matters more than the child's behaviour.

2. She made it safe for the family, holding back judgements and critical words.

3. The relationship, not the behaviour, was the highest priority.

4. As a leader, she walked the talk of connectedness the right way—through warmth, affection and attention.

14. Nurturing potential the RIGHT way

If we do not open our hearts to kids, we are not putting our best selves out there.

—Jen Bacus

Relationship needs to be at the heart of our work as educators. It is imperative that we ground our work in solid relationships, act from a place of understanding and empathy, and find comfort in our role as nurturer, mentor, guide and model.

Junior learns to fly

by Lis Kroeker

It was a beautiful early summer's day when I went to let my two golden retrievers out to the yard. It had rained at night, and the air was crisp and fresh. In the back yard, we had six big cedar trees that provided us with the sense of being in the woods. In addition to providing us with shade, they housed a number of creatures that provided entertainment for our family. Among the inhabitants was a family of Stellar Jays. We had watched them build their nest early in the spring, had waited eagerly in anticipation of the little baby birds and had been serenaded by their songs early every morning.

What I didn't know when I opened the door to let the dogs out was that the Stellar Jay family had decided that this was the day that junior would learn to fly. Junior didn't look very junior any more—in fact, he was now larger and louder than either of his parents, who faithfully spent the day feeding him and nurturing him in preparation for this grand event—the day he would fly! Except that he didn't fly. He jumped out of the nest and landed right in the middle of the yard, only to be spotted by my golden retriever who immediately moved to do what she was bred to do: to retrieve the bird that lay helplessly and loudly on the ground. This all happened within seconds—the door opened, junior jumped and fell, the dog ran and retrieved, and a cacophony of screaming from junior, his parents and me filled the yard!

Thankfully, my golden retriever had learned to do my bidding, so she immediately dropped junior and came back into the house, as commanded. My heart pounded as I quickly moved over to the window, wondering if junior would survive this ordeal. After loud screeching and much hesitation, junior was coaxed back on to the tree where he spent the rest of his day jumping (flying?) from branch to branch.

When I look at my teenage children, I can't help but think of junior. They are large, loud and very confident. They assure me that they can fly, but I know that my job is not over yet, that I still need to hold on to them as they practise moving from branch to branch until they really are able to fly!

Lis's story highlights much of what we explored in Part 1:

1. To raise a child is to nurture the full potential of a human being.

2. Maturation is the process by which potential is realized. Our role in this developmental process is one of cultivator.

3. It is our responsibility, and ours alone, to cultivate a secure relationship with the child, such that he/she is at a place of rest. This will provide the space for his development. If the child is at rest, nature will do the rest. This is assuming, however, that the child has trust in the relationship, that he/she can adapt when things do not go his/her way, and that there is tolerance of vulnerability.

Here is another story that speaks to our role as the cultivator of a child's development:

The way to face a bear

by Lis Kroeker

"The way to face a bear is to look it straight in the eye and yell 'I'm not afraid of you, you silly old bear'," Luke said confidently to his friend, John, as they stood on one of the logs at the back of their campsite. Luke was six years old, and full of life, emergent energy and imagination. For a child his age, a small wooded area can become a grand forest full of beasts to be conquered. A rock by the water is a giant cliff to be climbed in order to find safety and a long-lost treasure. A small creek is a wild river to be crossed.

What Luke didn't appear to be aware of was that his father was sitting only six meters away, watching him. Because he usually felt extremely safe with his father, Luke was able to lose himself in his world of adventure. André, his father, delighted in watching his son—ready, should he require support, yet letting him go so he could develop. Bowlby (1988) states that those children who are most stable emotionally and who make the most of their opportunities are those who have parents who, while always encouraging their children's autonomy, are available and responsive when called upon.

I am always struck by this concept. The more secure the base for the child, the more he/she is able to venture forth. We may think that we need to jump in and instruct children, telling them what they ought to do if they encounter a bear. Yet the most precious gift that we can give them is to encourage them to venture forth, while we remain close by, at the ready, should they require or request our assistance.

I am challenged by this notion, as a mother. Yesterday, I watched my son go to his first high-school dance. He was so excited he could hardly contain himself. He fretted about the dance all week, talking about what he would wear (I thought this was something only girls did!) and talking about who he would hang out with. While the kids had their dance in the gym, the parents were invited to an orientation to the secondary school, in the library. I listened to the principal and the teachers talk about their programs, their opportunities, their expectations and boundaries, and I wondered... and I feared. Will my son be ready for all of this? Will I know how to let him 'venture forth', yet be near enough to provide him with that secure base so that he has a place to 'come home to' when he needs it?

Key points

1. Lis made room for her son's budding individuality—his preferences, opinions, judgements and decisions.

2. She did not abandon her role as nurturer and protector.

3. She allowed her son the freedom to be himself, in the context of loving acceptance.

As we work to develop the whole child, we must be purposeful and intentional about nurturing each child's unique 'spark' (see Benson, 2011). Our challenge lies in identifying what sparks a child and what his/her inner light is. We must ask ourselves: *"What brings a child joy? What sparks his/her engine? When is a child at his/her best? How can we celebrate his/her special capacities—gifts that the world needs?"* We must name, know and nurture his/her sparks.

We must also ask ourselves what our vision is and what aspirations we have for our children. As committed connectors, we must aspire to nurture children who:

1. are seen and heard, belong to their family and their school community, and feel significant, loved and known;

2. are anchored with their families, have champions and are nurtured;

3. are engaged in their school and in their community;

4. contribute and are thriving;

5. embody kindness and compassion; and

6. experience joy, hope, direction and purpose.

Furthermore, in order for us to truly nurture children, we will need to be:

1. settled and grounded ourselves;

2. anchors for children and youth;

3. engaged at home and at work;

4. kind and compassionate;

5. valued and acknowledged; and

6. connected with people and things that provide hope, strength and comfort.

I encourage you to take inventory and to reflect on your 'spark biography' by asking yourself the following questions:

What is my spark?

What was it when I was 16 years old?

Has it changed?

Where do I express my spark?

What stands in the way of me expressing my spark?

The **RIGHT** model[20]

The time is right to charter a new course in education, for us to step up and step in! It is time for us to invest in people, not things. It is time to build capacities in children and each other and to deliver the proper goods: people connected to others and engaged in their community.

It is time to do the right thing—to get it right, and for the right reasons. At the core of the RIGHT model are these 12 tenets:

1. Focus on compassion to make the world a better place.

2. Empower teachers by providing scheduled, structured collaboration time for taking action.

3. Focus on student/teacher relationships.

4. Be intentional about aligning school and community leaders/ structures.

5. Build on existing strengths and strong roots—such as community schools and neighbourhood houses.

6. Engage in joint initiatives with community organizations.

7. Develop clear and regular communication with parents.

8. Take the time to create opportunities for students to have input, contribute, and take ownership of their learning. Identify meaningful support and pathways.

9. As part of a comprehensive educational program, design and implement unique and specialized programs to meet the needs of learners.

10. Introduce programs to strengthen capacity for caring and compassion.

11. Enhance the personal development of the child. Find the spark!

12. Create a culture of care. Produce graduates who will serve their communities.

---

20   Ogilvie, 2012

Connectedness at both the classroom and the school level begins with good role-modelling. The time is right to put connectedness at the centre of our school growth plans. It is time to shift from 'ill-being' to well-being. It is time to speak and teach the language of connectedness—the language of quality. It is my hope that the RIGHT model inspires you to champion the cause of connectedness. I hope it takes you back to the basics, to what is sacred, to our humanity, and to our hearts.

R – relational; right relationships; richness (when we/children/ communities are at our best)

I – intentional; inclusion; invitation; in person; interactions; integration; inside out; identification (of sparks); inquiry; involvement

G – gratitude; gifts (that we/children bring); getting back to basics; getting rid of what doesn't work

H – health (promotion); hope; heart; human spirit

T – thriving; trust; togetherness; thinking (outside the box)

Keeping our eye on the ball

How do we keep our eye on the ball, on linking people in a common journey and on strengthening families and communities? Here are five strategies:

1. Build/draw on the examples of inspirational leaders.

2. Invite colleagues and community members into dialogue. Problem-solve on how to build community.

3. Build a culture of trust. Trust in the expertise, professionalism and passion of all partners and in their ability to follow through.

4. Through stories, programs and materials, open up physical, virtual, familial and organizational spaces where connectedness can be explored.

5. Steer away from typical fact-filling processes and towards a relationship-building process.

We must remind ourselves of our mission. What are we doing to bring a child into connection with us? What are we doing to deepen our relationship with each other? Are we speaking the language of quality relationships? Are we child-friendly and family-smart? Are we doing our best to build the strongest organization of all—the family? Are we being purposeful and intentional about:

- sparking kids;

- celebrating their special qualities;

- recognizing the gifts they bring to our world, how they light us up;

- appreciating their gifts, much needed by the world;

- showing we care;

- helping them to feel that they belong and are significant; and

- building ConnectZones that foster a positive learning environment, promote open communication, and engage students, family and the community in decision-making processes.

15. Harnessing the power of connectedness

This is about figuring out how to
be a better human being.
Your job is to know that your
most powerful field is love; to give love,
share the love, be the love.

—Oprah Winfrey

To harness the power of connectedness is to be in the lead. It is to make a commitment, an intention, a promise, to stay in charge, to stay generous, to take care of another who is in a dependent position. It is all about the child and the connection.

Being in the lead has you reading the child but not giving the lead away. It is about staying close and paying attention to the child, taking the initiative and always being available to listen or offer support. It has you focusing on the following 3 Cs: context, compensate, correct:

Context (of connection within which to work)

Focus on:

- cultivating and preserving the relationship;

- how to be (not on what to do);

- how to reach them, first;

- having soft hearts;

- the relationship more so than on the incident; and

- being the caregiver, the cultivator.

Compensate (for stuckness and resulting problems)

Work around problems and address the underlying dynamics by focusing on:

- changing circumstances to take control;

- freedoms and expectations (working within what the child is able to do);

- structure and routines to create order (not to boss the child around);

- special traditions and celebrations;

- letting it sink in when things are not working (adaptive functioning);

- giving commands the child can follow;

- being proactive, not reactive;

- anticipating problems;

- collecting the child before directing; and

- backing off until you have a better hold.

Correct (the root of the problem)

Remove impediments to maturation and development (which softens their hearts/defences) by focusing on:

- good intentions;

- coming alongside;

- helping the child to feel his/her frustration and to move from mad feelings to sad ones;

- precipitating sadness and taking the time to go into it;

- decreasing pressure of coercion, force or leverage;

- repairing damage done by counterwill fall-out (child has felt coerced or pressured);

- debriefing, when the time is right;

- getting the child to depend on you (take the lead);

- using a connecting tone;

- drawing out mixed feelings (instead of demanding self-control);

- going deeper (bearing in mind that behaviour is just the symptom);

- getting in touch with our own frustrations; and

- creating order based on their minds, not on their behaviours.

We harness the power of connectedness by taking the lead and having complete faith and belief in a child's potential. We discover the impediments to the child realizing his/her potential and remove them. We help a child feel his or her frustration and let it sink in, which is the essence of adaptive functioning. We, as adults, believe that children need to feel fundamentally safe in their relationships with us.

Our job as adults is to take the initiative to connect with children. I tend to think of connectedness as a one-way street. Children should not need to invest lots of energy in winning us over. Instead, we need to relieve them of this concern. It is not their responsibility to connect with us!

The following story illustrates how crucial it is that educators instinctively guide and direct, lead and look out for, take the side of, protect and defend the children in their care. It highlights how hard educators work to ensure that kids fit in, feel at home, are 'a part of' things and feel significant.

The first day of school

by Lis Kroeker

With a tummy ache, and trying not to disturb the household at 2:30am, my daughter paced the halls of our home last night in anticipation of her first day in a new school. I noticed the lights were turned on, and I knew in my heart that something was wrong. I went to her and I held her, and she shook and cried, and talked about her fears. What if nobody liked her, what if her teacher didn't invite her to exist, what if they wanted her out of the school?

As I held her, not taking away what worried her, but acknowledging her experience, I wondered how many other children were experiencing the same feelings. We send our children to school in September with the anticipation that they will be loved and safe, with the hope that whoever ends up teaching them will have a sense of regard for them and nurture their development.

I asked my student teachers this morning to think about the most memorable and special year when they were growing up and the role adults played in making this memory. Here are some of the elements that they identified as they reflected on how their teachers had helped them to feel safe and successful:

The teacher...

1. demonstrated genuineness by:

    • not being afraid to have fun
    • showing vulnerability
    • being real with the students

2. demonstrated unconditional positive regard by:

    • being attentive to the child
    • demonstrating caring
    • being in tune with the needs of the child
    • providing time outside of the classroom (or offering generosity of time and being together)

3. created a safe environment:

    • that was respectful
    • where the teacher acted as a model and took the lead
    • where variety and differences were valued
    • where mistakes were considered a learning opportunity
    • where the adult was approachable
    • where no questions were rejected or shunned
    • where the child was more important than rules or routines

4. fostered an atmosphere of belief in the child by:

    • setting high expectations
    • protecting the child
    • not giving up on the child when he/she was struggling
    • supporting the child in his/her struggles

16. Just say NO

Our lives begin to end the day we become silent about the things that matter.
—Martin Luther King

Have you ever attended a meeting about a child wherein those involved seemed stuck in a cycle of frustration, caught in a vortex of shame, guilt or anger, and bickering, bullying or taking sides rather than coming alongside the parent? Haven't we all, at some point, entered such meetings with an agenda—one that dismissed the child/parent—and sat in silence while some injustice occurred?

All too often, our school-based resource team meetings, collaboration meetings, parent meetings and meetings with community members involve adults who are far away from their soft hearts. These adults often appear imprisoned by their judgements, steeped in practices that shame and blame.

We need to say "no" to these kinds of meetings. Standing up and speaking out follows the recognition that something is wrong—and that means trusting our inner voice. Coupled with our collective power to hold others (including leaders) accountable for their actions, we are saying, "I see, I care and I will speak out in the child's best interests." In so doing, we are demonstrating genuine caring and respect for self and each other. We are modelling the cornerstones of healthy relationships: empathy, limit-setting, accountability, and loving communication. We are modelling what it means to be allied professionals.

A few months ago, I attended a school-based parent meeting that prompted in me some internal shifts that I could not initially make sense of. I recall being particularly annoyed at what I perceived as the school's agenda to convince a refugee mother that her child was too 'out of control' to attend school. Equally concerning to me was the fact that folks were not attuned to each other, that injustices were happening and that the decisions being made did not take into account the wishes of either the parent or the community partner. I recall noticing the parent's feet under the table; they were not touching the floor at all. My heart sank as I realized that the parent was not grounded or emotionally present in the meeting.

At that point, I felt compelled to speak up, suggesting that, while we were stuck and trying to make sense of the situation and how to progress, we should slow down, settle, breathe, feel our feet on the floor, feel our bums on our seats and tune in. I am happy to report that we came to a peaceful, collaborative and collegial solution that saw the child attending school where the parent was studying ESL.

That story highlights the need for us all to be bold and fearless, at times—to take on issues and situations that many in the system might view as 'off limits'. It's also a reminder of the importance of bearing witness to our inner processes and struggles, and to giving ourselves permission to feel and be in the struggle, to make room for conflictedness and to be patient with it. Out of this state of confusion will come calm, a greater sense of awareness and increased confidence. It means acknowledging negative emotional states, inviting them in and sitting with uncomfortable feelings. This is how we manage these situations!

Meetings can best serve as forums for re-engaging adults with children and each other in a way that facilitates deeper growth and maturation. For example, I might say to a parent: "This is not what you wanted for your child...this isn't working for you." Here, the emphasis is on the adaptive process, on the language of frustration, on coming alongside the parent and seeing him/her in a new light.

Finally, we need to say "yes" to meetings and processes that support and repair trust. We need to say "yes" to meetings that emerge and propel us forward to a new understanding of the importance of being in the lead with kids—of being their anchors and compass points. Meetings can help adults discover their essential ground, their vital connection and, from this foundation, their pivotal role as parents and caregivers.

Essentially, we need to say "yes" to meetings that are all about helping parents and each other form a new version of who we are and how we see ourselves. We need to say "yes" to practices and processes that:

1. radiate warmth and unconditional positive regard;

2. do no harm;

3. enable us to revel in the happiness of others and experience joy;

4. no longer hold us captive in our judgements about right and wrong, good or bad;

5. value intuition and insight;

6. tolerate ambiguity and not having the answer right away;

7. investigate how to cultivate connections with children and families;

8. explore how to stay in relationship with children and not go into survival mode;

9. discuss ways to preserve contact and connection so that children can feel safe enough to feel deeply, to talk to you and want to please you;

10. examine how to use connection instead of separation;

11. delve into how to create community yourself, as the adult; and

12. explore ways to get community members working together.

17. Breaking free of the old, staying mindful of the new

To get what you've never had,
you must do what you've never done.
—**Brian Tracy**

In the current education system, the focus is on shaping or sculpting the child so he/she behaves and fits in. Adults are the judges of how acceptable the behaviour is, and the process is one of learning, not maturing. If the circumstances are not conducive to healthy development and maturation, a child may never truly grow up.

The good news about practising connectedness is that we know, intuitively, how to do it. We can break free of old habits simply by following our intuition and helping children to fit in and reach their full potential. What we need to remember is that growth is less about behaviour and more about nourishment.

Keeping our sights on nurturing a child to maturity will keep us from getting bogged down with non-compliant, disrespectful, aggressive aspects of their behaviour. Focusing less on behaviour and more on emotion actually results in better behaviour. The essential element for the child is receptivity; for the adult, it is warmth. Keeping integrity with the purpose is all about coming from the heart, which requires lots of patience on the part of the adult.

To break free of old habits, it may be helpful to sketch out a strategy for taking back your classroom, which might even become the focus of your professional growth plan. You might simply ask yourself: *"What two things can I do this year to break free from old habits?"* or *"How can I be more attachment-friendly and developmentally safe?"* Focusing on practising just two steps will give you the confidence to make bigger breakthroughs later. You may think of this in terms of a yoga class. On Day 1, you might simply focus on one posture. You have to start somewhere!

For you, breaking free may be all about wellness, about living your best and having fun. It may be about cultivating better thoughts. Instead of thinking, *"I cannot do this!"* you might think, *"I am doing this!"* You may wish to practise 'out-of-the-box thinking' to move forward with building relationships—perhaps empowering friends and colleagues to do something for others to overcome isolation, or just doing something simple, such as placing your hand on the arm of someone in emotional distress.

To break free, mindfulness is often the key. Studies have shown that mindfulness reduces stress, chronic pain, depression and anxiety. Living mindfully, being aware of what you are doing, is essential before you can make changes. As someone who is often on autopilot, I have decided to live in the moment so that I can experience a sense of peace. Rather than spending much of my life worrying about the past or fretting about the future, I am mindful of every passing instance, which is helping me to be non-reactive, non-judgemental and non-emotional.

Breaking free, for you, may mean acknowledging that you no longer want to focus on children's deficiencies and inadequacies. Instead, you may simply see their resilience and grace. You may feel deeply blessed to have children in your life, and you may choose to focus more on nurturing those valuable relationships and on bringing about renewal from the inside out.

Alternatively, breaking free may be about being able to adjust to circumstances, focus on gains rather than losses, and feel gratitude. It may be about appreciating your blessings, your will and your skill. These are signs of resilience or psychological health. A resilient person is like a rubber band, capable of being stretched almost to breaking point but still able to snap back and retain their integrity. Resilience comes into play when you're under stress.

Studies find that if you're resilient, you recover from stress faster, reducing the damage it can do to the body. Resilient people learn to:[21]

- value themselves;

- look for measures of their success, not failure;

- adapt to change easily;

- feel in control of their lives;

- bounce back after difficult times;

- have close, dependable relationships;

- remain optimistic even in the face of change;

- function well under pressure;

- have a sense of humour, even under stress;

- have a sense of confidence and strength in themselves as individuals;

- believe that things happen for a reason;

- handle uncertainty or unpleasant feelings;

- know where to turn for help;

- like challenges;

- enjoy taking the lead; and

- have hobbies and other activities.

---

21   Harrar and Gordon, 2009

Remember these key guiding principles

Even if you have little resilience, you can take steps to build it and add to your toolkit. Here are some helpful tips for becoming more resilient:[22]

- Laugh at least 5 times a day.

- Don't panic.

- When adversity hits, take a deep breath, think about the situation and then list 5 things you can do without falling apart.

- Say to yourself: *"In the near future, this will be worked out/get better."*

- When problems occur, take control of the situation by asking lots of questions. Obtaining sufficient information and having options allows for integrative functioning, tempering you and enabling you to develop responses that will allow you to bounce back.

- Identify one positive thing in every situation.

- Manage your expectations—for example, if you expect everything to go perfectly, you are setting yourself up for disappointment.

- Recognize what you can and cannot control.

Growth is the outcome of rest, not work. We need to make room for the cycle of rest and must find the time and place for it. Our brain and our body require lots of rest for us to be our best and to allow the parasympathetic nervous system—the system of rest and recovery—to do its work.

We must realize that time takes time. Becoming a designated comforter for many of our vulnerable children is a very slow process, and children may not necessarily believe that we are genuine just because we are adults. (Kids have BS radar!)

---

22   Harrar and Gordon, 2009

We need to remind ourselves that disconnection is the underlying issue in the majority of problems we encounter in our families, schools, communities and organizations. Consequential actions cannot fix this. The answers do not lie in the incident; they lie in the relationship.

As connectors, our best tool is our insight. Our intent is to open eyes, not provide a prescription. Our role is to make it easy for kids to depend on us. Children must feel safe in order to be dependent, and they are more likely to do so in the type of school culture that champions kindness, generosity, calmness, collaborative problem-solving and connectedness. As connectors, we champion a culture that:

Moves away from	Towards
Reactivity	Receptivity to the range of possibilities
Resentment	Resilience
Silos; focus on me	Healthy, cohesive communities; a focus on us

To create a context of connectedness, we may need to soften children's hearts, summoning up initiative and ingenuity to win them over. We may utilize a dog, a horse, a toy or something shared in common (sameness). We get in the lead by putting on the saddle or the leash. The following story by a kindergarten teacher illustrates how effectively this can work.

Welcome to kindergarten
by Gayle Hernandez

At our 'Welcome to Kindergarten' event this year, I had the opportunity to engage in amazing ways with two incoming students. Both Dan and Todd were clearly uncomfortable with the event.

When Dan was invited to sit and listen to a story-reading with the rest of the children, he retreated to the back of the room without Mom and

133

sat with a group of adults. He crossed his arms and looked at me as if to say, "I'm not coming... what are you going to do about it?" I told him that we would miss him at the carpet and I was worried he wouldn't see the pictures so well, but staying where he was would be okay. When the story-telling began, I sought permission to sit beside him.

"Only if you need to," was his reply. I told him that I was worried about kindergarten, since I was new to the school myself and would appreciate someone to sit beside, but that I would not sit with him if he didn't want me to. He replied, "If that would make you feel better." I accepted the invitation and enjoyed the story alongside him.

The librarian then brought out a second Piggy story to share. I exclaimed, "Oh, Dan! This is one of my absolute favourites! I have to go and sit on the carpet so I can see the pictures better and would really appreciate someone like you to come and sit beside me to help me feel better." Dan didn't walk, he *ran* to the carpet and we had a few lovely moments together as he lit up and laughed through the entire story.

Todd and his parents arrived late to the event. Mom and Dad were clearly uncomfortable. Todd was even less comfortable. He came in, sat on a chair, and hugged a huge teddy bear that was almost as big as him. The bear was tattered and had clearly been well loved, over the years. I couldn't see Todd, just the bear. I went to shake hands with this lovely bear.

"Hello, I'm Ms Hernandez... and you are?"
Todd replied, "Bear."
"Pleased to meet you, Bear. I would be so excited if you could join us for kindergarten in September."
Todd: "Bear can come?"
"Of course, I would be disappointed if Bear didn't come.
Todd: "Will there be a chair for bear?"
"Of course," I said.
Todd's little eyes then peeked out and, slowly gaining confidence, he replied, "Then we can come."

Part 3. Creating a ConnectZone: a connected school community

18. Creating moral and civic habits of the heart

Education's highest aim is to create
moral and civic habits of the heart.
—Charles C. Hayes

Schools play a central role as laboratories for acts of conscience. Habits of the heart such as courage, goodness and compassion are shaped over a lifetime. They define individual conscience and determine how a person responds to others' pain or victimization. Developing students' hearts is what educators are called to do.[23]

The primary challenge facing schools is moral illiteracy. Many schools place minimal emphasis on graduating people of conscience who are inspired to act for a higher purpose and to do what is right. It is not uncommon for schools to prohibit students from practising civic habits of the heart, getting involved in social or civic engagements, or contributing to a cause.

Schools need to focus not just on budgets and test scores, but also on creating climates of compassion and service. To prepare students to be ethical, engaged citizens, we must provide meaningful opportunities for them to practise shared decision-making, social justice, civic responsibility and service learning. They need to be given a meaningful voice in shaping the life of the school. Character education not only gives students a sense of belonging; it also transforms an entire school culture. With it, members of the school community are enabled to feel like part of a caring family.

---

23   Hayes, 2009

Educators are compelled to engage their students in projects and internships, in issues of social justice and civic responsibility so that they can discover a world bigger than themselves and a desire to make that world a better place. Through character education and civic learning, students are taught the skills needed to participate as effective and responsible citizens. Only then can there be a moulding of civic conscience. Only then can schools become laboratories of democratic freedom, committed to preparing students to stand up for liberty and justice for all. The following is an inspiring account of how one school has created such a culture.

Educating the whole child, at Byrne Creek Community Secondary School

by Dave Rawnsley

Byrne Creek Community Secondary School in Burnaby, BC, won the prestigious ASCD Award for Education of the Whole Child in 2012 (the only Canadian school to ever do so). Here, the school staff and community are committed to moulding a civic conscience, educating the whole child and engaging students in learning that is deeply related to the world around them.

Byrne Creek is a diverse and complex school. It is located in a lower-to-middle-class socio-economic area of south Burnaby that has undergone great change over the past 20 years. The 1,250 students at Byrne Creek come from 50 countries and trace their cultural heritage back to 20 more. Sixty percent of the students in the school have learned, or are learning, English as a second language. Over the past seven years, over 600 government-assisted refugees have settled in the Byrne Creek Community. Many of the students from these families have arrived in Canada after being uprooted by war in countries such as Afghanistan, Iraq, Iran, Sudan and Somalia. Some have never attended school, while others come from highly educated families that have been driven from their homeland by political strife. The journeys they have experienced are often painful to hear about and difficult to comprehend. Without exception, this transition is a true test of resilience and perseverance. Once in Canada, many of the students and families struggle with their new western world and a potential loss of cultural identity. They are also faced with a daunting economic reality, an uphill battle into a rigid and inflexible education system, and a profound gap between the academic challenges students face each day and the academic pressures and expectations their parents have for them. At Byrne Creek, these students join a complex blend of Canadian-born students and international students to form a vibrant and dynamic learning community.

The diversity at Byrne Creek creates a richness and energy that is second to none. It has also manifested a mindset among staff that is rooted in deep caring and a commitment to student safety, character and civic education. For teachers looking for a predictable place to work, Byrne Creek is not their school. Teachers are daily faced with the daunting task of helping students to achieve authentic success, while creating an environment in which students can find their voice through their own experiences and, despite their vulnerability, maintain a clear vision of themselves as thriving learners. For some of the school's most vulnerable learners, this can be a monumental task. Consequently, teachers have become masters of differentiation and personalization. They seek to understand each individual and account for all aspects of a student's development in a thoughtful and integrated way. In many cases, this begins with the provision of some very basic needs.

Byrne Creek has a breakfast, lunch and after-school food program to ensure that students have the nourishment required to go about their day. The school also has community partnerships that enable it to offer fresh fruit and vegetables, bread, and dairy products to families in the community. There is also a clothing program that provides jackets, gloves, socks and other clothing items to families requiring support. The school offers a comprehensive program of counselling and social services to students and families to ensure a strong fabric of social-emotional health. These services include counselling for post-traumatic stress disorder (PTSD), mental health, and drug and alcohol addiction, in addition to settlement services, parent education programs and career planning.

The success of Byrne Creek has not occurred by chance. The importance of community, dialogue and care has been reflected in the development of the school since its initial design. The school is a warm, welcoming facility where students, parents and staff feel safe. It has large open spaces for community gatherings, a 120-seat Centre for Dialogue modelled on the UN General Assembly, open hallways and bright, natural light. The school offers a broad range of programs designed to challenge students and prepare them for post-secondary study and success. It has a comprehensive range of courses at all grade levels, including Honours, Advanced Placement, adapted and modified programs. There are vibrant Fine Arts programs in areas such as dance, drama and music; innovative studies in technology and media; comprehensive athletic and intramural opportunities; and Industry-Connect programs that allow students to gain dual credits while earning formal industry experience and certification.

Byrne Creek's motto of HEART—Honesty, Empathy, Achievement, Respect and Teamwork—is displayed in the atrium for all to see and is embedded in all aspects of the school community. In a survey conducted for the school, over 90% of students reported feeling safe at school. In the same study, over 85% of students reported feeling close to people at school, part of the school, happy to be at school and treated fairly by teachers at school. All of these results are above the provincial and national averages.

The school staff have designed a flexible timetable that affords students the opportunity to access learning at all times of the day and in various forms. This timetable allows families to create schedules around family and work commitments; enables students to maximize their exploration of areas such as community outreach, performance arts and athletics; and creates the opportunity for students to blend traditional 'bricks and mortar' schooling with online options and to study alongside parents in our Continuing Education programs.

Since the school opened, teacher collaboration has been a structured part of its practice and culture. Each week, teams of staff meet to discuss student achievement and develop support plans. In doing so, teachers review the school's broader goals, assess progress and adjust instruction to ensure that they are supporting students in the best way possible. As an extension of the work undertaken in collaboration time, staff members have formed cross-curricular learning teams. These teams work with district program consultants to identify best practice in a specific area and implement strategies in their classrooms. One concrete example of this commitment to collaboration, community and student connections is the development of Byrne Creek's 'village', which is a group of staff that have formed partnerships with families and community members to create a web of support around some of our most vulnerable students. The 'village' meets weekly as a large group to discuss issues, research and progress. Smaller support teams meet on an ongoing basis to develop more explicit support plans for students identified as being vulnerable or at-risk.

Byrne Creek's commitment to social justice, civic responsibility and service learning can be seen in a broad range of programs in the school. The Byrne Creek Leo Club is one of the largest school-based service learning and volunteer groups in North America. This group provides students with the opportunity to apply their learning, reinforces responsible citizenship, and helps develop sustainable living and leadership initiatives throughout the school and community. Byrne Creek's Independent Directed Studies program provides an opportunity for students to deepen and broaden their learning in an area of interest. It also offers the potential for truly personalized learning, as it enables students to connect their current studies to their own journeys and previous learning, enhance opportunities for service learning and give them a voice in developing their educational experience.

The most powerful example of developing the character, conscience and heart of students at Byrne Creek may be The Paving a Way for Success (PAWS) program. PAWS was originally developed by school staff to support immigrant students who entered the public school system in

Canada late in their high-school years. The program provided targeted workplace learning opportunities and community connections to develop reading, writing, numeracy and workplace skills. Over the past two years, the program has built on this foundation, evolving into a comprehensive program in partnership with the school district, Immigrant Services and Mosaic Cultural Services (a multilingual non-profit organization dedicated to addressing the issues affecting immigrants and refugees in the course of their settlement and integration into Canadian society). It continues to provide wrap-around support, essential skills and incremental workplace training. Students selected for PAWS work with staff to develop a personal learning plan. Through the development of the plan, each student's academic, social, emotional and personal journey is explored. This process helps establish the foundation upon which future goals and objectives can be built and learning can take place.

The PAWS program is divided into two distinct phases. In the first phase, students concentrate on achieving personal successes, uncovering skills, goal-setting, communication and safety skills. In the second phase, students expand on their learning through community work experience placements. During the work experience, the students are supported by an employment coach and youth and family worker in developing their skills for the job. These work placements allow students the opportunity to practise English in a meaningful context, learn about Canadian culture and acquire work-related skills. Students are also encouraged to participate in community activities to improve their language skills. The PAWS program has had a positive impact on the lives of students at Byrne Creek, with noticeable improvements occurring in all measurable areas of knowledge and skill development. Most importantly, there has been a marked improvement in students' confidence and a strengthened connection between the students, their families and the school.

The overall success at Byrne Creek is the result of passionate staff, thoughtful planning and integrated programming coming together in a vibrant and diverse community committed to habits of the heart. The staff members at the school are dedicated educators who genuinely care for students and approach each new challenge with an open mind. They love teaching at Byrne Creek and view every decision through the lens of what is best for our kids and our community.

The school has the active support of the Burnaby School District and community in planning in a thoughtful, proactive and integrated manner. As a result, they have been successful in responding to the needs of students, making adjustments when necessary and moving forward in a consistent and sustainable way. They are particularly proud of how our entire community continues to deepen and broaden its understanding of what it means to educate the whole child and how they have been able to make a lasting difference in the lives of their students.

19. Igniting the community moral purpose

There is never an excuse for
treating anyone with disrespect.
—Jim Dillon

Adults may not see the issue of connectedness as applying to them. Perhaps parents and students do not view it as their problem. What I would like to see is students and adults working together as partners in building ConnectZones. Students are often viewed as the problem and not the solution. They are turned off by negative messages implying that they are to blame for many of the problems in schools. The following approaches can help us to move beyond just solving problems and to ignite the community moral purpose of creating a positive and supportive school culture.[24]

1. Tell a different story. Re-frame issues so they do not become another problem on a long to-do list. Having a positive school culture is at the core of every school's educational mission.

2. Stand on principles. It is crucial that schools invest the time to determine, articulate and communicate guiding principles for how all members of the school community should speak and act. Explaining the reasons for these rules is important.

3. Make all students valuable in the eyes of their peers.

4. Establish trusting relationships with all members of the school community.

5. To strengthen the school community and plan for the next steps in the process, include all members of the school community in the process of determining guiding principles.

---

24   Dillon, 2013

6. Translate guiding principles into specific words and actions— for example, build trusting relationships with students by greeting them by name as they walk into classrooms.

7. Align adult behaviour with principles. We must model the change we want to see.

8. Empower students to feel a sense of ownership for their school community.

9. Believe that change is possible.

10. Read and discuss research on how people change.

One of the ways I have endeavoured to model a relationship-centred approach to education is through building and mounting effective collaboration. I started with weekly school-based collaborative sessions at an elementary school, which later extended to bi-weekly sessions for high-school educators within the same zone in my school district. This initiative, named Collaborative for the Study of Connectedness in School Communities, now brings together representatives from surrounding school districts for bi-weekly sessions to discuss their journey towards connectedness in their school communities. A common theme in this process has been that their journey towards connectedness in their school community has been a worthwhile one.

20. Guiding connectedness through mentorship

*Our world does not improve because
people complain about their lives.
Our world improves because people take
responsibility to improve the lives of others.*
—Patti Hill

So much has been written about the benefits of mentorship. Perhaps you look back fondly, as I do, to those who impacted your life in significant ways. I warmly remember my first days as a high-school counsellor in Burnaby, British Columbia and my early conversations with Alice Kozier, a school principal. She was amazingly talented at getting the most from her staff. During my first conversation with her, she welcomed me to her school and gave me permission to do what I do best—connect with people. She spoke the language of quality, kindness and generosity. She acknowledged my inner light, my spark, and then proceeded to ask me to bring joy, hope, direction and purpose to members of her school community. To top this, in only our second meeting together, she nicknamed me 'Ogles'. I felt that I belonged and that I mattered to her. In an e-mail to her, 25 years later, I thanked her for her leadership, for making me feel welcome and significant, and for mentoring me like no other.

As stressed throughout this book, our education system is predicated on wanting kids to comply, obey, fit in and follow. Educators are preoccupied with teaching the curriculum. Many of us have become obsessed with prevention programs and data collection. While I acknowledge the merits of empirical evidence, I worry that we may be over-emphasizing the importance of data collection, while losing sight of what is really important: that we are teaching a child—that there is actually a person there!

I worry that many of us are deeply 'in our heads' and too far away from our hearts. Perhaps we insist on, and find comfort in, the notion of healthy boundaries and keeping children at a distance. Some modern practices that have become the expected norm among staff (such as duty-free lunchtimes) have, arguably, resulted in teachers spending less time with kids, less connection and less mentorship. We've got to get back to the basics—to reaching kids before teaching them.

Steve Cairns poses some key questions, in this respect: "Where do we 'reach' our students? At the door, when they arrive? How about at the crosswalk? Do we take a little walk with them down the block and back before and/or after school? During recess and lunch hour, are we in the hall or on the grounds? Are we trying to reach kids through an activity or club, for fun? These are the roots of belonging and loyalty. And how about connecting with parents, just for the sake of it? Are we informing parents when things are going well, when their children are doing the right thing with peers or school or self?"

This chapter delves into the importance of connecting with parents. Without a doubt, our world is being shaped by the relentless advance of technology. We live in a world of infinite information via the Internet, which offers enormous opportunities for learning. Personally, I am challenging myself to change my fundamental views about connectedness and am beginning to see the possibilities for technology as a human connector. I also see, however, a need for more human acts of compassion and connection. To this end, we are called upon to:

1. **inspire** a shared vision for school connectedness;
2. **nurture** a health-promoting school environment;
3. **model** the way for respectful, supportive relationships;
4. **challenge** the process to be one where kindness is valued and practised;
5. **enable** others to act more interpersonally, to build community;
6. **encourage** the traits of compassion, integrity, gratitude, authenticity and humility;
7. **become** a mentor; and
8. **ensure** that every student has a mentor.

Mentorship is basically an invitation to exist—to participate in something. It is about emergence, about acknowledging a child's curiosity, interest, talent or something you share in common (sameness). By teaching the child about a particular issue or skill, and by sharing resources and networks, the adult facilitates the child's growth and challenges the child to move beyond his/her comfort zone.

I recall a story of musically inclined teachers mentoring students by inviting them to jam with them on the weekends. Later, they invited these students to join them in their professional gigs on stage. Personally, I find comfort in the knowledge that having my nephew join me on the golf course when he was just 12 years old was a key factor in his decision to take up the game seriously and secure scholarships at a prestigious university. He eventually went on to join the PGA tour and achieve success as a professional caddy.

I think of mentorship as training wheels on a bike. When children fall off the bike, we've got to be their training wheels. It's our job to run alongside the bike to help them develop their balance. They find comfort in knowing we're close by, guiding and balancing them. This may mean directing them down a particular path, or maybe taking the lead and inviting them to join us on our stage.

I feel compelled to continue Peter Benson's legacy. He stressed that youth are not vessels to be filled but fires to be lit. Innovation—the best of development—comes from the inside out, not the outside in. Benson used the metaphor of the 'spark' to describe the animated engine, the inner light, the bringer of joy, hope, direction and purpose to the child. He sought to understand their spirit—what was going on when they were their best and happiest.

We must help kids to identify, name and nurture their sparks. Benson's formula for human thriving involves identifying kids' sparks, having three adult champions to nourish these sparks, and creating opportunities to pursue them. In close alignment with Benson's philosophy, I yearn for the day when kids' sparks become the topic of our first parent meeting at the beginning of the school year and for it to be at the forefront of our mission in schools and our school growth plans.

The following story is about children and youth following adult cues, with adults modelling desirable actions, preserving connection and promoting maturation.

Grade 8 rugby: a story of mentorship
by Wade Wilson

In my second year of teaching, I was assigned an alternative education class for at-risk youth, Grades 8–10. When four out of my six enrolled students decided to join the Grade 8 Boys Rugby team, I knew I had to find a way to participate. Part of my reason for becoming involved was because I foresaw difficulties arising from them all being together. The regular rugby coaches were already at a loss as to how to deal with the behaviours that were springing up, and we were only two practices in. A few of the boys were being targeted and picked on; others didn't have a clue as to how to play the game. For several of them, this was their first time being involved in a team sport at school and I feared that the experience would be negative and, in all likelihood, turn them completely off team sports.

So I started co-coaching rugby. I had a relationship with all boys and my presence helped mitigate some of the bullying and swearing that was running rampant among them. Many of them were highly defensive and reactive and were more focused on counter-attacking than learning the drills and skills required in rugby. I noticed an immediate change once I started showing up. They were able to see me in a different role than that in which they saw me in the classroom. They were able to witness that I was athletic and, consequently, developed a new respect for me. I was modelling the roles that they were interested in. Rugby also allowed for acceptable physical contact for all parties involved. They got a chance to try to tackle their teacher, which they quite enjoyed but, given my prowess and strength, my leadership role was naturally augmented.

Despite the rough start to the season, the students settled in and became more comfortable with each other—on and off the field. They had shared experiences and, whether they realized it or not, they had become a part of something bigger than just themselves. Too often, children become insular and withdrawn because every time they extend themselves beyond their comfort zones, their initial experiences are negative. Having another adult to coach/police is beneficial but having an adult/mentor participate in the things they voluntarily join makes the students feel as if you're becoming a part of their lives.

Since then, I have made it common practice to involve myself in the activities in which they are interested, whether that means bringing my gym strip to school so I can go to the weights room with them, or going jogging, swimming or hiking with them throughout the year. I cannot promote community and school involvement, or active and healthy living, unless I take the students by the metaphorical hand and show them how it's done.

Wade clearly influenced his students and used his relationship with them to articulate his values and promote desirable behaviour. For his part, it involved careful nurturing, trust and a strong belief in the power of relationship, all of which motivated the students to perform.

I'm reminded that connected kids:

1. like school;
2. feel they belong;
3. believe they are cared about;
4. believe that education matters;
5. have friends at school;
6. believe discipline is fair; and
7. have opportunities to participate in extracurricular activities.

21. Inviting parents into the connectedness process for optimum results

Nothing about parents without them.
—FORCE Society BC[25]

Educators acknowledge that an important ingredient for their students' success is a strong working relationship with the parent. What follows is a story that demonstrates the value of this, as well as the need to keep our connections with students strong.

A mother's story

(anonymous)

When I brought my son to his first day of kindergarten, I had the same hopes and dreams as every parent. I wanted him to be happy, to make friends and to do well in school. Throughout the years, I learned that my dreams and reality were not always aligned and that my ultimate role as a parent was to support and advocate for my child. As a teacher and staunch supporter of the education system, this was often my greatest challenge.

In my son's first three years in elementary school, there were signs of difficulty that I often minimized or overlooked. I knew my son was bright, but focus was always an issue. He was struggling to acquire reading and writing skills and was becoming increasingly frustrated and shut down in his classes. At the end of Grade 2, I challenged a teacher who had labelled him passive-aggressive, which resulted in an ideal Grade 3 placement for him with a teacher he had success with. To this day, when I'm asked about

25   www.keltymentalhealth.ca

teachers who made a difference, his Third-Grade teacher's name is the automatic and only response.

During the summer before Grade 4, we moved to another school and community. My son became involved with sports, made friends at school and daycare, but he missed his old friends and his school challenges continued. He was diagnosed with a learning disability in Grade 5, but strategies and expectations remained the same. He often asked me if he could be home-schooled and/or come to my school, but I resisted, largely because I was concerned about the judgements of my colleagues. His intermediate years were particularly challenging because of the emphasis on academics. He started missing a lot of school due to illness (mainly gastrointestinal issues).

During the summer before high school, I was advised by a professional, who had identified that ADHD was a probability, to approach the school and explain my son's need for support. When I did, I was told that this was high school and it was time for me to step back and let him take responsibility. At some level, I was relieved to follow this advice because the fighting over schoolwork at home was becoming intolerable. His attendance was problematic but he was able to pass all subjects that year.

Near the end of the first semester of Grade 9, I was informed that my son's attendance was minimal and that he was failing most subjects. Thus began a series of calls and meetings with various members of the staff and school-based team. Most of our discussions focused on academic deficits and emotional concerns. During one meeting, I was asked, "Do you think he's normal?" I was perceived as part of the problem and many discussions were focused on my son's emotional/ mental health and my parenting. Life at home was volatile and our arguments were escalating physically and emotionally. We were both out of control and I felt desperate, afraid and alone. I knew that we needed help. The school year was lost and my son had been informed that he would be repeating Grade 9. I sent him on a 30-day wilderness course for troubled teens. We both needed a break and he came back strong, optimistic and refreshed.

In spite of my son's good intentions, within several weeks of his second attempt at Grade 9, old patterns emerged. He was offered academic support, but there were no strong connections with staff. When I asked the counsellor for the name of an adult in the school who would be able to connect with my son on a regular basis, his response was, "I suppose that would be me, but don't expect it to be every day."

As a parent, I was becoming increasingly uncomfortable every time I entered the school. I could feel eyes roll as I entered, and the conversations were never positive. I will always remember the first meet-the-teacher night of the second Grade 9 year. It was like speed dating—five minutes with each teacher. I heard about a litany of failures. Several teachers were unaware that this was my son's second year at this grade level and the PE teacher skipped the greeting and simply said, "Your son is failing my class." By the time I reached the music teacher, I was defensive and unprepared for his compassionate comments. "How is your son doing? He is such a natural and talented musician." I burst into tears and thanked him. I apologized for my emotions and told him this was the first time in a very long time that anyone at the school had said anything positive about my son.

Things continued to deteriorate. I was introduced to the school psychologist, who, because of my persistent questions about educational concerns, had done a file review. She discovered that the former assessment I kept referring to was missing from the file and she questioned the validity of the most recent assessment. She agreed to maintain the learning disability designation but only if I agreed to an H designation (severe behaviour and/or mental illness). Even as a teacher, I felt I had no other options and I capitulated. A short time later, my son was asked to leave.

During the exit interview with the principal, he asked me, "As a parent, how was your experience at our school?" I responded, "Honestly, I felt judged and blamed." His response to me was, "And so did we." I do believe my son is an educational casualty but it would be too easy to place all of the blame on the school system. Based on the lessons I have learned, I recommend that parents do the following:

1. Choose a school where there are positive connections for students as well as parents (a 'village of attachment').

2. Listen generously to your child, the teachers and yourself (trust your instincts).

3. Nurture your child's interests/passions. Acknowledge and build on his/her strengths.

4. Leave your ego at the door. Forget about what others will think.

5. Avoid attending school meetings in an emotional state. If you do, bring a trusted listener.

6. Be clear about what it is you want/need. Present it in a way that can be heard.

7. Work *with* the school team, not against it.

8. Don't hide or work in isolation. Ensure that there is a circle of support for child/parent.

9. Know when and how to ask for help.

10. Ensure that relevant information is shared with the appropriate teachers and staff. Never assume that it has been.

11. Enjoy the journey.

As demonstrated in that story, coming alongside parents, and planning with them about their child, is an area in the education system where we are definitely receiving a failing grade. All too often, we plan about them without them. We do not honour their intuitive language—that is, knowledge that is sensed or unconscious. Often we do not trust their empathy for, or understanding of, what their child needs. We rarely acknowledge them as 'expert' and as 'being in the lead'.

What role do we play, on behalf of parents?

I believe our primary purpose is to empower and serve as connectors when meeting with parents. I often ask myself these essential questions when interacting with a parent:

1. Do I operate in a manner that doesn't dumb the parent down?

2. How can I work to understand a parent?

3. How can I work to see a parent differently, without trying to change her/him or be overbearing or judgemental?

4. How can I be there to truly listen to a parent—to cultivate a connection with her/him and validate his/her feelings?

5. How can I make it safe for a parent to ask questions and empower them to ask the right questions?

6. How can I avoid accusing a parent, in any way, and instead solicit their input and help?

7. Am I quick to judge?

8. Where do my regular conversations about/with parents lead?

Through all of this, it is vitally important that we have the intention of building a good relationship with the parent. We need to remind ourselves that parents are not there for us to unload our frustrations upon, or to disrespect, bully or disempower. They are, in fact, our valued partners. We need to thank them for inviting us into their confidence and for sharing their story with us. We honour and safeguard them and invite their partnership when we ask questions such as these:

- Is there any advice you can give me as his teacher so that I can...?

- I need your help so that I can teach your child better. Do you have any suggestions/ideas as to how I could do this?

- How can you help me understand your child better?

- At home, what works for you when...?

In the process of building relationship with parents, our focus is on coming alongside them as our equals—as partners and co-facilitators in the development of their child. We strive to preserve their dignity and honour them as experts in taking the lead with their child. This allows us to endear the parent to the child by showcasing the child's wonderful qualities/talents. In so doing, we show the parents that the more they invest in their relationship with their child, the less time and energy they will need to spend on dealing with adverse behaviours.

Today, in order to forge stronger partnerships with parents and to strengthen communication with relevant community agencies, many school districts are offering parent information forums related to positive learning environments. Schools are using communication technology, along with traditional approaches, to improve the flow of information between schools and homes. Many teachers are using technology to provide timely updates about children's progress academically, socially and emotionally. Many send photos with these updates to provide an immediate glimpse into the school day or use classroom blogs to document the learning experience. Websites are utilized to post resources and assignments and to communicate with students and parents. Teachers are now including parent resource packages on their sites, showing parents how they can better support their child's learning. School principals and district superintendents are updating their websites, sending out e-bulletins, and publishing blogs to share their insights into the workings of the school/district, highlight upcoming events and recognize accomplishments.

Students are more likely to succeed when parents take an active interest in their children's education. Parent engagement is key to student success and this can only happen when parents are in the loop about what is happening in the classroom and the larger school community.

There are definite benefits to a more proactive approach to communicating with parents, whereby parents are invited to engage and offer their support, while students, teachers and administrators contribute blog posts about what is going on in classrooms and school communities. Collaborative conversations about education are happening with the broader community, and this open, transparent approach to communication is creating more supportive learning communities.

Coming alongside parents

The following two stories by Lis Kroeker speak to the important issue of honouring parents' intuitive language and knowing, while acknowledging parents as experts in taking the lead with their child. More importantly, they speak to our true role as connectors and our purpose when meeting with parents.

And a shoe came flying by...
by Lis Kroeker

I was sitting in my office helping Jake with his math when I heard the sound of crying coming from down the hall. It was dismissal time for the kindergarten students, and the hall was full of parents getting their little ones ready to take home. We looked at each other, shrugged, and kept on working. I figured that there were lots of other adults in the building who could take care of this. However, minutes later, a child peered into my room and asked me to come and help. I asked Jake if he could get himself back to his class, and rushed down the hall to see what was happening.

There is a certain fear that lives with me every day as a school counsellor. When all else fails, there is this strange expectation that the school counsellor will know what to do. I suppose that, after many years of schooling and extensive reading, I do know what to do, but only to a certain point. Life is unpredictable and, no matter how well we understand things intellectually, there is no telling how we will react in a crisis. As I ran down the hall, wondering what was awaiting me and silently praying that I would know what I needed to do, I could hear a teacher talking about 'that parent'. "That parent doesn't know what to do. If she only stopped indulging that child and set some boundaries, we wouldn't have this problem! You have to teach her to manage this child!" As I entered the room, I heard her say, "I can't stay, I have another appointment."

There, in the middle of the room, was a young mom on her knees, gently rubbing the back of her daughter, who was clearly distressed. Mom looked up at me, her face full of shame. I stepped forward slowly, but not slowly enough. The little girl looked at me, panicked, took her shoe off and threw it at me. I had overstepped her boundary, but now I knew what to do!

I found a little chair, sat far enough away so both the mom and child would feel safe, yet close enough to establish a connection. Quietly, I started to chat with the mom about her child, nodding, listening and affirming, as much as I possibly could, that this mother was in fact taking the lead for this child and following her heart. As we chatted, we realized that the child was extremely sensitive, and that she often became overwhelmed by her environment, experiencing a vulnerability that was too much to bear. I didn't need to talk to this mom about setting boundaries and managing her child. All I needed to do was affirm to this mother the rightness of following her parental instincts in caring for her child.

The thing is...
by Lis Kroeker

"The thing is," whispered the father slowly, "there is something wrong with me." I sat across the table from this large, strong, rough-looking man, not quite sure what it was that he had come to speak to me about.

His son, an active and highly alarmed little six-year-old, was having trouble in our school. He had come to our school full of fear, unable to settle down and seeming to struggle with understanding what was happening around him. His mom had told us two years ago that his father was out of the picture, and we hadn't really asked any more about it—until recently, when the mom announced that she had lost her job, and that her ex-husband would be looking after the kids while she looked for employment.

Joey was struggling with staying at school for the whole day, sometimes becoming so alarmed that he would run into the forest. So the school started to call the parents at lunchtime to pick Joey up and take him home. I am not sure if this was meant to be a punishment or a break, for Joey. One day, Joey's dad appeared at the office to pick up his son. He was calm and gentle with Joey. He thanked the teacher for giving him some work for the afternoon and told Joey that they would be working on this once they got home. Joey cried and screamed that he hated him. Then he ran off to the playground and sat on the bench, looking away. His father just walked over and told him that it was time to go home. Joey followed him to the car and they drove off.

"I don't know what is wrong with me," Joey's father told me. "Sometimes, I can't understand why I am not angry like other guys. They stalk their girlfriends, they beat them up but I... I just feel so sad and I cry. And then it is over and I don't feel anything any more." I looked at him and asked him to tell me more. "Men don't cry; that's what is wrong. I'm supposed to be angry, but I cry and then I don't want to be angry any more. I just want to make things work for my kids."

He talked about his kids and about the structures and routines at home. He talked about how important it was to follow through with what he promised. He talked about being with them. When I told him that his kids were lucky to have him as their dad, he teared up and told me about his conversation with Joey that day when he had picked him up. "The thing is," he said to Joey, "I am your dad and not your friend. And it is my job as your dad to make sure that you learn everything that you need to learn so that you can make it on your own when you grow up. And even if you don't like what I tell you that you need to do, you are just going to have to trust me, because I am your dad."

Key points

1. The secret of a parent's or educator's power does not lie in formal training, a set of skills or techniques.

2. Fundamentally, what matters is our relationship with the child.

3. Children need to be taken care of, to feel that they belong and that they matter.

22. Watching them flourish

Only understanding can dissolve
stuckness and facilitate change.
—**Bev Ogilvie**

In the next story, Lis models the reality that parenthood is, above all, a relationship. As the story indicates, her children count on Lis for guidance. They lean on her with their emotional needs. The ingredients fundamental to making parenting work are all there: a dependent being willing to be taken care of, an adult willing to assume responsibility, and a working attachment between the child and the adult.

The big fat 'F'
by Lis Kroeker

"I'm afraid that your son has only completed 8% of his assignments in English, and he is looking at a 'fail' on this report card," said the teacher, over the phone. "We tried keeping him in at lunchtime for detention to motivate him, but it appears that he just does not care about getting his work done."

My heart sank as I heard these words, and I felt guilty as a parent. Why didn't I see this coming? I had asked him every day if he had any homework; I had seen him working in the office... why hadn't I been more on top of it? Needless to say, I didn't sleep all night, worrying about him, worrying about his future, and worrying about what else I had failed to do as a parent to prepare him for this world.

I chatted with him about the problem. He felt bad about the hole that he had dug himself into, but didn't seem to know how to get himself out of it. I asked him to ask the teacher for a list of every assignment that was missing (I also e-mailed the teacher, asking him for the list) and, once we had it, I asked my son to talk to me about each of the assignments. I got him to ask for clarification on the ones he did not understand. Then we prioritized them—the ones that would require a lot of work and planning, and the ones that he could complete in a short while. We then took each assignment and put it in the calendar so that he could plan what he would tackle each day to get caught up. He had three weeks of school left; the goal was to have everything in to the teacher in two weeks.

I stationed myself, with my computer, in the same room as him, while he was working, partly because I wanted to make sure that he was staying on task, and partly because I wanted to be able to help him if he got stuck. I noticed that it made a difference to him that I was there. At first, he kept asking me for help, but then he started to work on his own, telling me that it really helped when I stayed with him. I promised him that I would be in the room working on my stuff every day that he was working on his. Each day, he got more done without needing my help as he became more confident about what he needed to do.

By the end of the two weeks, my son had handed in every assignment, and we got an e-mail from the teacher saying that he would be passing English after all. It occurred to me that what my son had needed was for me to move closer again, to lead him through the process. It wasn't that he lacked motivation or didn't care. He didn't know how to get going; he needed me to take the lead. It reminded me of when he learned to ride his bike. At first, he avoided the topic of bicycles altogether. Then he insisted that I run next to him, holding on to the bike. Slowly, I let go of the bike seat and just ran along with him with my hand close to him in case he lost his balance. One day, I stopped running and watched him take off!

Recently, we were working in the office. This time, my daughter was with us, working on a science project, and my son was working on an assignment due the following Monday. I was also working on a project. It occurred to me that this was where I needed to be—close to my kids as they evolved in their academic learning, sometimes running along and sometimes just watching them as they took off, but being there, nevertheless.

The key theme of this book is that children are meant to be raised in the context of connection. This is where the real power to raise a child resides. The more you work with this power, the more you will see how people naturally respond, and the more you will want to use it.

To me, connectedness makes the world go round. It brings out your creativity and helps everyone around us flourish—ourselves, our children, our students and our colleagues. It engenders hope, it softens our defences and it frees our hearts. It rekindles our inner light and allows us to feel joy. Our power comes from who we are, not from what we do or what we have. It allows us to say "no" out of love, rather than "yes" out of fear.

Connectedness is a matter of worthiness. Children learn that they are worthy of many things—of telling the truth, of helping others, and of belonging in their school and family. They learn that they are sacred in their own right and capable of reaching their full potential.

Our best hope of building vital connections with children is not only to understand their developmental deficits but also to recognize their emotional reality and, in particular, their desire to connect. So often, our interactions with children are goal-directed—that is, we want them to do something, and much of our day is spent telling them what that is. We should not be surprised, therefore, when children become angry and frustrated, because all they really want from us is to feel valued and connected.

If we want a kinder, more caring society, we need to provide children with more experiences and places in which they feel safe. To encourage compassionate action, we need to create conditions and emotional states conducive to it. If we want to combat bullying, we need to focus on connectedness and belonging. If we are concerned that social media are undermining relational health, we need to be purposeful and intentional about building resilience through consistent, high-quality personal relationships.

Although I worry that social media can create relational conflict, isolation and a loss of face-to-face connections, I acknowledge that it can increase relational richness by linking friends and family over distances. It can create new connections when used in addition to, rather than a replacement for, in-person contact.

To combat the alarming trend of disintegrating social fabric, we need to do the following:[26]

1. Spend more time with our children.

2. Encourage spontaneous self-motivated play—especially outdoor play, as it is vital for healthy social and emotional development.

3. Ensure that our children have well-developed social and emotional skills.

4. Value kindness and empathy. Respect our need for connection.

5. Increase engagement through volunteering and mentorship.

6. Promote volunteering as much more than a requirement for college admission; rather, it is an opportunity to make a difference, to give back to the community and to increase engagement and contact with all ages.

7. Have explicit discussions around perspective-taking (how others may perceive things differently), body language, facial expressions and tone of voice, to help children deal with social signals.

8. Promote empathy.

---

26   Perry, 2006; 2010

9. Discipline with reasoning, consistency and love.

10. Be responsive, verbal and sensitive. Use our words to help children use theirs.

11. Encourage children to think about those less fortunate than them and how they can help. Get them involved.

12. Have explicit discussions about how people's actions affect other people and why others might have different points of view.

13. Rather than using discipline, use class/family meetings to talk about what really matters.

As parents and educators, we need to insist that our school boards and leadership teams make healthy relationships a priority. Is connectedness a core mission? Do our systems and practices show respect for relational health? Do they reflect the reality that we need more empathy than ever before to deal with today's complex challenges? Do they promote happiness? Is psychological health modelled at central office? Do our leaders recognize the importance of having ConnectZones in order to support staff in meeting the diverse needs of children and youth?

Humanizing school cultures is our most powerful way of preventing and reducing disengagement and disconnectedness. We must not forget that our absolute presence, in and of itself, is often enough to bring about a sense of community in others.

I wish you much success in your endeavours to walk the talk of connectedness in schools. May you harness the power of connection and find comfort in speaking up and out for kids and families. May you find the voice to pay tribute to them and to recognize and celebrate their worth. May you experience connected, reciprocal relationships and feel invigorated by them.

I leave you with my personal recipe for creating your own ConnectZones, in as many ways and in as many areas of life as you feel inspired to do.

Bev's recipe for humanizing work, cultivating hope and shifting your life:

1. Get engaged in a network and community of practice. Give back to your community.

2. Highlight gender equity and inclusion, while helping to minimize all forms of segregation.

3. Practise gratitude by having family gratitude rituals, keeping a gratitude journal, and using gratitude jars (write a short note daily about what you're grateful for and place it in a jar; if you are having a bad day, open the jar and read a note).

4. Be kinder and gentler with yourselves and each other.

5. Talk to yourselves the same way you'd talk to someone you care about. Practise self-compassion.

6. Be mindful of your negative emotions. Avoid getting caught up and swept away by negativity.

7. Be willing to be vulnerable, as it allows you to live and love wholeheartedly.

8. Live a life defined by courage, compassion and connection.

9. Practise the 4 Rs: rest, relax, recharge and refresh

10. Cultivate meaningful relationships.

23. Summary

This book has focused on the following key teachings:

1. Relationships are essential to human development.

2. Connectedness leads to better emotional and physical health.

3. The motivation to form and sustain social connection is one of the most powerful, universal and influential human drives, shaping emotion, cognition and behaviour.

4. It is essential that we provide children with the tools to help them understand and regulate their own emotions, build confidence and improve academic performance.

5. Even the best policies, programs, rules and protocols will fail unless they can take root in a positive, caring school culture.

6. Programs teach children skills, but we must change their hearts. This involves much more than stopping a negative behaviour; it means cultivating a school community in which everyone is treated with warmth, respect, honesty and compassion.

It has also touched on many of the wonderful activities that schools are doing to become more caring and respectful communities. I hope that it has mobilized and inspired you to become involved in warding off a culture of disengagement in our schools, to turn to one another in support, comfort and connection, and to proactively make a difference in people's lives.

Appendices

Appendix 1

10 reasons to adopt a connectedness approach

1. It's an intuitive, heart-centred approach based on insights and a healthy way of thinking (not a method or a set of prescriptions).

2. It's about realizing human potential.

3. It enshrines the natural processes by which all of us grow, develop and mature.

4. It explores the deficiencies and dysfunction that result from developmental arrest.

5. It uses language that is common and closer to natural intuition.

6. It focuses on what is natural rather than what is normal.

7. It gets to the roots of behaviour (the beginning, the etiology) by making sense of it from the inside out.

8. It steers us away from medical or behavioural models and builds on a child's assets/spark.

9. It treats parents as equals, with respect and dignity.

10. It creates relationships that are nurturing.

Appendix 2

How to cultivate connection

- Recognize that attachment is the most powerful force of all.

- Perceive the child as being in need of the adult. Create a safety net for the child.

- Invite parents/adults to offer their care and expertise. Solicit the child's good intentions.

- Collect, bridge and matchmake.

- Be in the lead, take over and look after the child.

- See and identify with the child's point of view.

- Stay the course; don't throw in the towel.

- Comfort children when they are wounded.

- Manage oneself rather than trying to manage the child.

- Create rituals/activities that embrace connection.

- Assume responsibility for the relationship and for preserving the connection.

- Take charge of decisions and circumstances regarding the child.

- Show the child that you have his/her best interests at heart.

- Create scenarios where the child can rely and depend on you.

- Normalize times of confusion and disorientation. Model mixed feelings.

- Soften defences first.

- Say "no" to the child, when necessary; set limits but help the child through times when things don't go his/her way.

- Help the child move from feeling mad to feeling sad.

- Prime the adaptive process. Consequences must evoke feelings of sadness and disappointment in the child.

- Focus on social and emotional learning.

- Build a culture of compassion and caring.

- Be a role model and a mentor.

Appendix 3

Wade's connection practices

The following are strategies used by a teacher to purposefully and intentionally build relationship with his students:

Introductory practices/activities (early in the school year)

- BBQs or picnics at parks

- Taking an interest in students' lives, questioning them and getting a sense of their history

- Connecting with parents through informal meetings, going out for coffee/tea/lunch

- Picking students up from home and dropping them off

- Walking them to their integrated classes

- Greeting them in the morning and asking how their night was, how well they slept etc

- Going on a team-building hike or other outdoor physical activity

Day-to-day practices

- Gathering them in the morning, with greetings, eye contact, undivided attention, handshakes

- Providing breakfast, lunch and snacks throughout the day

- Phone calls in the morning (wake-up calls)

- Using humour and joking with them

- Constant communication with parents and outside agencies

- One-on-one sessions, walking, running, drives, schoolwork
- Making connections with the larger peer group
- Making smoothies
- Playing games with them (checkers, connect-4, cards, dice, spoons)
- Working out with them in the weights room/recreation centre, playing basketball, badminton
- Getting the morning paper and going through it with them, sharing news, sports, horoscopes
- Taking student concerns to their regular teachers and becoming their advocate
- Sharing moments of undivided personal attention
- Reminding them they have unique skills and qualities
- Hugs, playful punches, neck and shoulder rubs
- Positive reinforcement

Weekly, monthly, special events

- Getting buns, bread and other snacks from community donations and delivering them to students' homes
- Special treats (icecaps, liquorice, ice cream)
- Playing practical jokes (such as April fool's)
- Going on monthly field trips (e.g., swimming, museums, hiking, go-carting, snow-tubing)
- Lending bus fare, small amounts of money
- Going shopping to buy things they need
- Sharing lunches

- Involving outside speakers and presenters on issues such as drugs, gangs and sex education

- Attending their extra-curricular events, Xmas concerts, sporting events

- Sending Christmas and summer care packages

- Coaching or co-coaching sports they are involved in

- Bringing them for haircuts or cutting their hair

- Staying in contact with ex-students and their parents

Emotional practices

- Building on their interests and creating lesson plans around them

- Telling them stories about our lives and the struggles and hardships we endured

- Accompanying them to places when extreme stress is a factor (counselling, programs, work places)

- Stating our feelings as the basis for why something should or should not be done

- Reviewing their behaviour with them and connecting it to how it makes them feel

- Goal-setting and creating visualization or dream boards

- Discussions on what makes them angry/frustrated, sad and happy

Appendix 4

Daily proactive school/class connectedness strategies for IEP/FBA

- Focus on creating safe and caring schools, with daily morning messages and whole school activities

- Morning check-in with adult

- Birthday announcements/class parties

- Community-building activities, with opportunities for child to work with a variety of class members

- Teacher to create systems for assigning partners and creating groups

- Positive behaviour notes: provide explicit feedback when students are seen to be following the rules

- Explicit teaching of class routines and expectations

- Teach sensory-based strategies for staying focused in class, and signal each transition with a one-minute brain break

- Teach self-regulation strategies, offering programs such as yoga and mindfulness

- Teach class visual problem-solving model (circle–square–triangle)

- Zones of Regulation program/other SEL programs such as Roots of Empathy

- Fidget tools for everyone and during group instruction

- Have a help card system: I need help with some of it/all of it/ one part of it (teacher to number steps on board)

- Leadership opportunities throughout the school (daily brain boost, recycling, school store, office monitor, safety patrol, etc)

- Bubbles analogy for personal space—used by all teachers in all environments

- Buddy readers; helper roles

- Breakfast club; food offerings

- 7–11 mentorship program (Grade 11 student paired with Grade 7 student)

- Individual sessions re: positive peer interactions, personal space and social thinking

- 2 x 10: teacher spends 2 minutes each day for 10 consecutive days connecting with child about topics that matter to him/her

- Social thinking, perspective-taking activities and vocabulary (focusing on expected vs unexpected)

- Individual session re: positive peer interactions, personal space and social thinking

- Small group work on special projects

- Front loading prior to challenging social situations

- Visual problem-solving model (situation, action, outcome)

- Assign older lunch buddy

- Assign high-school, university or community mentor

- Friend-to-friend friendship tips

- Each child has one designated school adult anchor

- Three community champions for each student

- Adults greeting students and parents

- Parents/community partners welcome/visible in school community

- Students involved in giving back to the community

- Students in helping relationships with others in the community, such as seniors

- Community outings

- Each child's spark(s) nurtured

- Special events that celebrate inclusion, equality, tolerance

- School teams/events/fundraisers

- Cultural celebrations

- Family night/movie night

- Special community forums/events to build connectedness, such as inviting community in to discuss how to build connectedness

- Greeting/goodbye rituals; smile/light up when we see children

- Match child with adults

- Bridge to high school by matching students with new teachers

- Make eye contact and greet each child by name

- Cultivate empathy

- Collaborative problem-solving

- Structures and rituals

- Comprehensive school counselling program

- Relationships, relationships, relationships...

- Sitting with people and hearing their story

- Compliment students in front of their peers

- Practise gratitude by journaling, filling gratitude jars, etc

- Focus on communities of care

- Steer away from separation/suspension

- Teach beyond the lesson plan, promoting community engagement

- Adults take the lead, making it easy for children to lean on them

- Walk child to class; collect him/her after disconnections/ transitions

- One-on-one support for students from support staff, including custodians, secretaries, educational assistants, community supports

- Movement breaks.

Appendix 5

A Network Connection Plan (NCP)

Date: _____

Child/youth: _____

Current anchors:

_____

Further anchors:

_____

Child's/youth's spark(s):

_____

Challenge/need:

_____

Behaviour(s) of concern:

Goals:

_____

Short term:

_____

Long term:

_____

Obstacles:

_____

Where are we going?

_____

What are we doing to purposefully and intentionally connect with the child?

_____

Identified strategies and tasks of adults

_____

Review date: _____

Glossary

Adaptive process: a natural growth force by which a child develops emotionally as a result of coming to terms with something in their life that cannot be changed. The child learns from his/her mistakes and benefits from failures.

Alarm: a hyper-aroused state of alertness, reflected in elevated heart rate, blood pressure and high activity. In extreme cases, may produce rage and sadness-filled tantrums.

Attachment: the drive or relationship characterized by pursuit and preservation of proximity—that is, movement towards physical, emotional and psychological closeness.

Autism Spectrum Disorder (ASD): a complex neurobiological condition that can affect the normal functioning of the gastrointestinal, immune, hepatic, endocrine and nervous systems. It impacts normal brain development, leaving most individuals with communication problems, difficulty with typical social interactions and a tendency to repeat specific patterns of behaviour.

Bridging: techniques used to help bridge separation, to retain an emotional connection.

Collaborative problem-solving: a compassionate, effective research-based approach to understanding and helping behaviourally challenging children and youth.

Collecting: a greeting ritual designed to get others to attach to us.

Connectedness: being connected to someone and feeling cared for and respected by them.

Counterwill: the human instinct to resist pressure and coercion.

Emergent process: a life process whereby an individual develops viability as a separate being—a 'venturing forth' energy, giving rise to a sense of responsibility, curiosity, boundaries, respect for others and individuality.

Empathy: connecting with the emotion experienced by another—the ability to stand in another's shoes, to see and feel the world from their point of view.

Functional Behavioural Assessment (FBA): an individualized and data-based collaborative process that brings insight and clarity into the reasons for challenging behaviour and how to teach and promote desired behaviours. Reveals information about the antecedents, consequences and frequency of challenging behaviour (contexts and outcomes of the behaviour) and the functions of the behaviour.

Individual Education Plan (IEP): a concise, useable, documented plan developed to support success for a student with special needs.

Integration process: a natural growth force that involves the mixing of separate entities to produce perspective, balance and emotional and social maturity.

Matchmaking: facilitating a relationship between a child and someone responsible, through introductions, compliments and friendly interactions.

Positive Behavioural Support (PBS): an empirically validated, function-based approach, founded on behaviour theory, designed to eliminate challenging behaviours and replace them with pro-social skills. (See FBA above.)

Resilience: the capacity to cope with stress and recover from adversity. Resilience is demonstrated through the ability to, for instance, be in charge of our emotions, reach out to others, empathize with them, and analyze the cause of problems.

Self-regulation: the ability to monitor, evaluate and modify one's emotions; sustain and shift attention, when necessary; and ignore distractions—the ability to understand and engage in social interactions in a socially appropriate way, connecting and empathizing with others.

Tears of futility: what we experience when things cannot or will not work. Involves feelings of sadness and letting go that are vital to a child's development.

Vulnerable: capable of being wounded. The human brain is designed to protect against vulnerability that may be too much to bear.

References

Abblett, M. (2011) The light at the end of the tunnel vision: Mindful limit setting. *Journal of Safe Management of Disruptive and Assaultive Behaviour*, 19:14-17.

BC Ministry of Education, Special Education Services (2013), *A Manual of Policies, Procedures and Guidelines*.

Benson, P. L. (2011) TEDxTC, *Sparks: How Youth Thrive*. See: http://goo.gl/bRISv

Bowlby, J. (1988) *A Secure Base*. Basic Books, New York.

Brown, B. (2012) *Daring Greatly*. Gotham Books, New York.

Burnaby School District Learning Support Services Manual (2005).

Dillon, J. (2013) Smartblog on Education, *Bullying prevention from the ground up*. See: http://goo.gl/zgy4XV

Goleman, D. (1996) *Emotional Intelligence: Why It Can Matter More Than IQ*. Bantam Doubleday Dell Publishing, New York.

Greene, R. (2005) *The Explosive Child*. Harper Collins, New York.

Greene, R. (2008) *Lost at School*. Scribner, New York.

Gruwell, E. (2007). *Teach with your Heart*. Broadway Books, New York.

Harrar, S. and Gordon, D. (2009) Are you resilient? *Reader's Digest*, pp158-159.

Hayes, C. (2009) Schools of Conscience. Educational Leadership. *Teaching Social Responsibility*, Volume 66, Number 8, pp6–13.

Kessler, R. (2004) Grief as a gateway to love in teaching. In D. Listor and J. Garrison (eds), *Teaching, Learning, and Loving: Reclaiming passion in educational practice* (pp137-152). Routledge Falmer, New York.

Neufeld, G. and Mate, G. (2005) *Hold on to your Kids*. Vintage Canada, Toronto.

Perry, B. and Szalavitz, M. (2006) *The Boy Who Was Raised as a Dog*. Basic Books, New York.

Perry, B. and Szalavitz, M. (2010). *Born for Love*. Harper Collins, New York.

Reicher, M. (2010) *Hopeful News on Teaching Boys: Exploring the Human Element in Teaching Boys*. Education Week (online).

Russell, S. (2013) Witnessing as short-term trauma support. *Insights into Clinical Counselling*, December 2013, pp32-33.

Schill, J. (2010) *The power of words*. CPI Instructor Forum.

Sinek, S. (2009) *Start with Why: How great leaders inspire everyone to take action*. Penguin Group, New York.

Wheatley, M. (2002) *Turning to One Another: Simple Conversations to Restore Hope to the Future*. Berrett-Koehler Publishers, San Francisco.

ISBN: 978-0-9879291-6-7